France from the Air

France
from the Air

PHOTOGRAPHS BY DANIEL PHILIPPE
TEXT BY CLAIRE JULLIARD

✳

*With 157 photographs in color
and 11 maps*

THAMES AND HUDSON

Translated from the French *La France vue d'en haut*
by Jane Brenton

Any copy of this book issued by the publisher is sold subject to the
condition that it shall not by way of trade or otherwise be lent, resold, hired out or
otherwise circulated without the publisher's prior consent in any form of binding or
cover other than that in which it is published and without
a similar condition including these words being imposed
on a subsequent purchaser

First published in Great Britain in 1997
by Thames and Hudson Ltd, London

First published in the United States of America in 1997
by Thames and Hudson Inc.,
500 Fifth Avenue, New York, New York 10110

British Library Cataloguing-in-Publication Data
A catalogue record for this book is available from the British Library

ISBN 0-500-01772-7

Library of Congress Catalog Card Number 96-61425

Printed and bound in Italy by Vincenzo Bona - Torino

Contents

Introduction

WHEN MONSIEUR SEGUIN'S little nanny-goat reached the top of the mountain she peered down into the valley below. 'It made her laugh till she cried,' wrote Alphonse Daudet. '"How small it is!" she exclaimed. "How could I ever have fitted into that?" Poor thing! Perched up there so high, she saw herself the same size as the world.' What an intoxicating sensation – the feeling of lightness and power we experience when we look down from above, our eyes skimming over roofs, fields and towns that look like a series of abstract mosaics. How amazed we are to discover new colours, the patterns made by fields, towns and watercourses. How exciting it is to find craters at our feet, to peer down into the ocean depths. ... For once it is not the creations of nature or man that tower above us, but it is we who are the masters of the elements. Two marvellous inventions – the hot-air balloon and the camera – have allowed this illusion of divinity to be restored to us.

At the end of the nineteenth century, the balloon acquired a new lease of life with the perfection of extraordinary devices for the recording of panoramic views – among them one designed by Monsieur Triboulet which could trigger the simultaneous release of seven shutters. The very first aerial photographs were taken by the great Nadar, introduced to ballooning by the Godard brothers. Today, the whole process has been made routine by the aeroplane and we can travel almost anywhere from the comfort of our own armchairs. Photographers have all the time they need to line up their shots, enabling them to offer a personal view of a landscape or locality. The photographs in this volume, by Daniel Philippe, have been chosen to reflect the 'geopoetics' of the artist rather than to give a logical overview. He has taken care to convey the stylistic profusion and character of the land of France – the works of nature and the works of man – combining the objectivity of the lens with his subjective viewpoint. Philippe has a particular angle on the world: a fortress amid the waves, a field or village clinging to the side of a cliff. Sometimes the images seem like a bewildering stream of *non sequiturs*, like imagination run riot or nature itself, rampant in spite of man's best efforts to impose order upon it.

In Gaston Roupnel's *Histoire de la campagne française* human endeavour is described as being 'always intermittent and random'. 'Man disperses and distributes his labours over space and time; his activity is fragmented and scattered among the exceptional places, the events and episodes of history. He always acts in obedience to the changing whims of the capricious personal genius he carries within him. And the works of his mind are by no means the least evidence of that capriciousness, that spasmodic quality of human labour.' Similarly, this book invites the mind to play with a landscape or a monument, it does not attempt to offer the exhaustive coverage of a guide. An image may spark a historical anecdote, a flight of fancy or an association of ideas in precisely that random manner that characterizes this genius. A particular shot may give rise to a digression on the ghosts of the Laestrygonian giants, or the Ankou rowing his silent boat over the Baie des Trépassés – from the Mont Saint-Michel to the banks of the Loire, from Alsace to the Pyrenees, stones and monuments tell their tale of the glories of French history. Through them we relive the ostentatious displays of the over-ambitious Fouquet at Vaux-le-Vicomte or of François I at Chambord, or the triumphant arrival of Louis XIV at Saint-Jean-de-Luz. One page closes on the fate of Louis XIV's queen, Madame de Maintenon, another on the memory of Diane de Poitiers. Hosts of images spring from the text as history becomes saga, with the arrival of the Vikings from the Atlantic, the demise of the last Cathars at the château of Quéribus, the Allied landings in Normandy. The land is still stained with the blood of the conspirators of Amboise, and of those who perished in the French Wars of Religion and the Normandy landings. The monuments are equally expressive: from the ruins of Vézelay to the architectural fantasies of Viollet-le-Duc, or the controversial Louvre pyramid.

Aerial photography, being essentially a poetic art, enjoys a particular affinity with literature – the texts here are augmented by literary portraits of France, incorporating quotations from the books that have made this ancient land familiar to people the world over, and have helped shape an identity, a language and a way of life. Thus, each region is introduced with an extract from a novel or an essay. What would the point be in attempting to express something a great writer has already said far better than we ever can? Are we to attempt to rival Flaubert and Maupassant with our descriptions of Normandy? Could we hope to evoke the sweet countryside of Touraine better than Balzac? Is there any way we could match the wit and panache of Vialatte – in his delightful chronicles of *La Montagne* at Clermont-Ferrand – with his punning references to 'monts chauves auvergnats'? All the old regions that make up our present country have been written about by great writers, so we should not deny ourselves the pleasure of reading them. Colette's Burgundy, Flaubert's Normandy, Nerval's Île-de-France and Michelet's Brittany are among the extracts that appear here.

This small anthology gives a flavour of great French literature – to quote from or refer to a particular poet is an expression of admiration comparable to the close study of a landscape or a photograph. References to writers also appear where relevant to individual pictures. Sometimes these are descriptions of the houses where writers were born, which they chose to make their home or in which they found refuge, like Balzac at Saché, Colette in her 'Treille muscate' at Saint-Tropez, Vailland at Meillonnas, or there are descriptions of writers setting off to travel round France, notebook in pocket. Thus we will see the young Flaubert traversing Brittany in the company of Maxime Du Camp, Stendhal visiting the Midi

to collect material for his *Mémoires d'un touriste*, Victor Hugo scaling the mountains of the Alps and Pyrenees – in the grip, as always, of blinding visions. We return frequently to Hugo in this volume.

Neither are artists neglected, for France has also provided the inspiration for innumerable paintings – Gauguin and his disciples wreaked merry havoc in Pont-Aven, Van Gogh captured Provençal light and colour, Signac, Modigliani and Bonnard all in their turn discovered Saint-Paul. Yet, it is literary France that holds pride of place in this anthology, whether as precise naturalistic descriptions or as imaginative recreations in the Proustian manner – the author of *À la recherche du temps perdu* invented a Normandy of his own, based on the very real memories of his childhood. In some way the atmosphere of the places he had known and the houses where he had lived lingered on in his memory, fuelling his obsessive explorations of the past. In the writings of the Romantics, in particular, the theme of the homeland plays an important part. Other authors such as Bosco, Giono, Daudet and Vincenot have made it the subject of their entire oeuvre. This literary genre has attracted the faintly pejorative and belittling epithet of regionalist, but it is an empty word signifying a total lack of understanding: each bit of the universe, each road and each stone has within it its own cosmogony in miniature. Bosco's mysterious low Provençal hills express all the magic of the world. They address us all 'in a language of personal accents' (Lamartine). This is why there are so many regions and remote corners of France which, even though we have never set foot in them, nevertheless look familiar when we see them in photographs. Let us hope that everyone leafing through this book will discover resonances of his own.

The North

and the Île-de-France

I AM SORRY TO LEAVE SENLIS, but my friend insists I follow up an idea I carelessly let slip. ...

I was so enjoying myself in that town where the Renaissance, the Middle Ages and the Roman epoch coincide, here and there, on a street corner, in a stable, in a cellar. I mentioned 'those ivy-covered Roman towers!' to you – the everlasting greenery that clothes them casts shame on the fickle nature of our cold lands. In the Orient, the woods are always green; each tree has its season for shedding; but that season varies according to the nature of the tree. So it came about that in Cairo I saw sycamores lose their leaves in summer, but they were green in the month of January.

Senlis is encircled by avenues, replacing the ancient Roman fortifications that once stood there – subsequently restored after the long residence of the Carolingian kings – and now there is nothing more to see than rusty leaves of elm and lime. But the view of the surrounding countryside is still beautiful, by virtue of a splendid sunset. The forests of Chantilly, Compiègne and Ermenonville: the ruddy-coloured masses of the woods of Châalis and Pont-Armé standing out against the light green of the fields in between. The towers of distant castles still stand, solidly built of Senlis stone, but generally used now only as pigeon lofts. The pointed bell towers that bristle with the regular protuberances that are called *ossements*, or 'bones', in this part of the world (I do not know why) echo still to the sound of bells that induced such sweet melancholy in Rousseau's soul. ...

So, let us make the pilgrimage we have determined on, not to see his ashes, which repose in the Panthéon, but to see his tomb at Ermenonville on the so-called Île des Peupliers.

The cathedral of Senlis, the church of Saint-Pierre, used today as a cavalry barracks; Henri IV's château built against the town's old fortifications; the Byzantine cloisters of Charles le Gros and his successors, there is nothing here that need detain us. ... It is time once again to make our way through the woods, despite the lingering morning mist.

We struck out from Senlis on foot, through the woods, happily breathing in the autumn mist. We had taken a route that led to the wood and château of Mont-l'Évêque. Ponds gleamed here and there through leaves whose red was heightened by the dark green foliage of the pines. ...

In the village we drank a local wine perfectly acceptable to travellers such as ourselves. On seeing our beards, the landlady said, 'Are you artists ... have you come to see Châalis?'

Châalis: at that name I thought once more of a time long ago ... when I used to be taken to the abbey once a year to hear mass and visit the fair which was held nearby.

'Châalis,' I said, 'is it still there?'

We went to Châalis to have a close look at the estate before it was restored. First you come to vast perimeter walls surrounded by elm trees; then on the left, you see a building in the style of the sixteenth century, probably restored later to echo the heavy-looking architecture of the small château of Chantilly. When you have seen the pantries and the kitchens, the flying staircase built in the reign of Henri IV conveys you to the vast apartments on the lower galleries, to the large apartments and to the small apartments giving onto the woods. I noticed a few paintings in frames, the Grand Condé on horseback and some views of the forest and in a low room, you can see a portrait of Henri IV at the age of thirty-five. It dates from the period when he knew Gabrielle, so probably this château witnessed their amours. The prince, who I find rather unsympathetic, spent a considerable amount of time at Senlis, especially when it first became his country seat, and over the doorway, above the three words: *Liberté, égalité, fraternité*, a portrait bronze of him may be seen that bears an engraved motto explaining that it was at Senlis that he first knew happiness – in 1590. Yet this is not where Voltaire chose to set the central scene, copied from Ariosto, of his amours with Gabrielle d'Estrées.

Do you not find it curious that the d'Estrées turn out to be related to the *abbé* of Bucquoy? This is nevertheless what his family tree reveals. ... I am not making it up.

Gérard de Nerval,
Angélique in *Les Filles du feu*

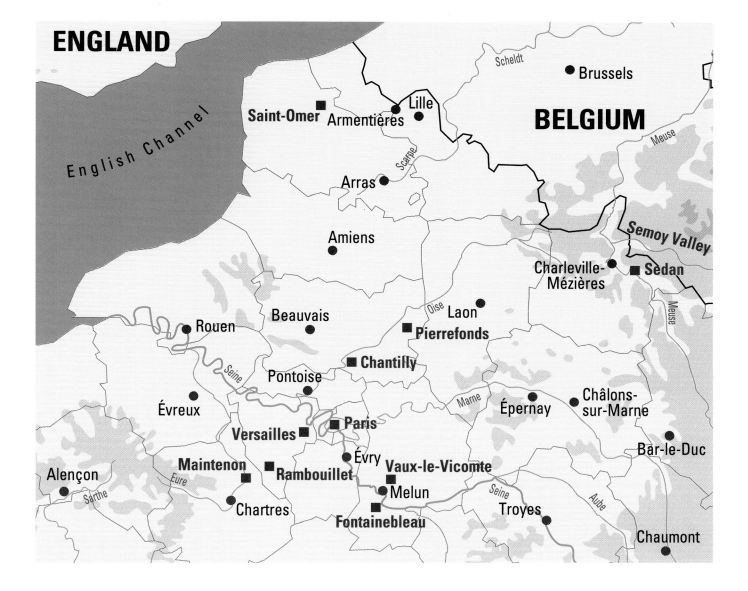

ENGLAND

English Channel

Scheldt

• Brussels

■ Saint-Omer
Armentières
• Lille

BELGIUM

Meuse

Scarpe

Arras •

Semoy Valley

Amiens •

Charleville-
Mézières •
■ Sedan

Meuse

Beauvais •
Oise
Laon •
■ **Pierrefonds**

Rouen •

Seine

■ **Chantilly**

Pontoise •

Marne

Châlons-
sur-Marne •
Épernay •

Évreux •

Versailles •
■ **Paris**

Évry •

Bar-le-Duc •

Alençon •

Eure

Maintenon ■
■ **Rambouillet**

Vaux-le-Vicomte
■ Melun •

Seine

Aube

Sarthe

Chartres •

Fontainebleau ■

Troyes •

Chaumont •

THROUGHOUT NORTHERN FRANCE, a marked Anglo-Saxon influence is apparent, even in the patois. For example, the marshes of Saint-Omer (*right*) are known as 'watergangs' or 'wateringues'. The Michelin Guide informs us these are the result of patient construction work started in the ninth century by the monks of Saint-Bertin. The waterways are ideal for peaceful boat trips and for catching tench, perch and roach. Migratory birds gather there. The place has a melancholy beauty of its own – often shrouded in damp mist, it evokes the atmosphere of a Simenon novel. But the region has another side to it – the green valleys and woodlands. The countryside of the North provides the ideal setting for the musings of the solitary walker. And anyone prepared to look for it can find the region's love of festivities. Someone somewhere is always celebrating something – whether it is at the local hop or the Dunkirk carnival, the people of the North know how to dance and enjoy themselves; on Sundays, pigeons are released in races called 'les coulonneux'. The area boasts a river with the name Aa, for which devotees of crossword puzzles should be grateful.

The quiet Semoy Valley (*above*).

MOST FRENCH PEOPLE, if asked to choose the two monuments that best symbolized their country, would mention the château of Versailles first and then the Eiffel Tower. Our sense of geometry is stirred both by the grandiose proportions of the palace of Louis XIV, the Sun King, and by the harmonious lines of Gustave Eiffel's famous landmark. Parisians generally use the arrival of a foreign visitor or perhaps a relative from the country as an excuse to arrange a visit to these two masterpieces. Originally, Versailles was no more than a hunting lodge, and then a place where receptions were held. When Louis XIV decided to enlarge the premises, in 1661, he commissioned the team responsible for Vaux-le-Vicomte: André Le Nôtre, who designed gardens, grottoes, lakes and waterways; the architect Louis Le Vau, who remodelled the main buildings and constructed one of the first 'follies', a Trianon of porcelain; and finally Charles Le Brun, who headed a group of painters, sculptors and tapestry weavers. After Le Vau's death, further extensions were undertaken under the supervision of Jules Hardouin-Mansart. The court, consisting of around three thousand people, finally occupied the various buildings and annexes in 1682. The lavish celebrations could commence.

MAINTENON (*left*) is the Renaissance château acquired in 1674 by Louis XIV as a gift for Françoise d'Aubigné, the future Marquise de Maintenon. She led an extraordinary life – orphaned at the age of twelve and with no dowry, she determined four years later to marry Scarron the poet, who was an invalid. Madame Scarron was widowed in 1660 and later became party to a royal secret, supervising the education of the bastards of Louis XIV and Madame de Montespan. When the king made one of them legitimate, with the title of Duc de Maine, the governess moved to court. Gradually she won the king's affections, overtaking many younger favourites. After the queen's death, Louis XIV married her in secret in the chapel at Versailles. She was then forty-eight years old. Her power over the king was undiminished until his death in 1715. A glittering destiny, perhaps, and yet this is the illuminating confession she addressed to Madame de Glapion in 1702: 'How can I make clear to you the boredom that gnaws at the great, and the difficulty they have in filling their days! Do you not see that I am dying of sadness surrounded by wealth you could scarcely imagine, and it is only with God's help that I am prevented from giving way? I was young and pretty; I tasted pleasure, above all, I loved; at a later time of life, I lived for years by my wits; I came to favour, and I assure you, my dear girl, that all these different conditions have left a terrible emptiness, anxiety and lassitude, a desire to experience something else, because in all of it there is nothing that is entirely satisfying.'

The fortress of Sedan (*below*) is the largest in Europe (35,000 square metres on seven floors).

THE ORIGINAL CHÂTEAU OF Pierrefonds dates from the twelfth century. It became the property of Philippe Auguste in 1181 and later passed to Charles VI, who gave it to his brother Louis of Orléans. When the latter became regent, he had the fortress rebuilt by the royal architect, Jean Le Noir. Pierrefonds was subsequently to hold out against sieges by the English, the Burgundians and finally the royal troops. Napoleon reacquired the ruins in 1813 and Napoleon III undertook its restoration. A keen archeologist, he entrusted the rebuilding of the keeps and annexes to Viollet-le-Duc in 1857. The work turned out to be more extensive than originally planned as the emperor decided to occupy the château himself. The architect then embarked on a complete restoration, taking a number of liberties with the medieval design. This provoked an enormous furore. He was accused of relying more on his imagination as an architect than on historical fact. Purists denounced his 'troubadour style', but children love this fairy-tale castle set amid the foliage of the forest of Compiègne. Its wonderfully cardboard-cut-out appearance has attracted a number of film-makers. In 1960, Jean Marais leapt gracefully from one of its towers in a famous swashbuckling scene in the film *Le Capitan*.

THE CHÂTEAUX OF THE ÎLE-DE-FRANCE are the jewels in the region's crown. Some, like Rambouillet (*below*) or Fontainebleau (*opposite*), are known principally for their forests and are much frequented by the public. For Parisians, they have tended to become synonymous with picnicking and Sunday walks. Fontainebleau conjures up the name of François I and that of a school of painting, but the château has existed since the twelfth century. Louis VII, Philippe Auguste, Saint Louis and Philippe the Fair all stayed within its walls. François I transformed the former medieval manor house into a Renaissance palace, entrusting the construction work to Gilles Le Breton. Under the aegis of the Florentine, Rosso, and Primaticcio, from Bologna, many artists laboured to make the buildings 'a new Rome'.

FRANÇOIS I's SUCCESSORS
redesigned the château of
Fontainebleau. Napoleon was
to prefer Fontainebleau to
Versailles (he was tormented
by the ghost of Louis XIV), and
(presumably as some sort of variant
of *noblesse oblige*) set his imperial
mark on it by embarking on yet
further improvements. Today,
Fontainebleau is a museum, while
Rambouillet has been the summer
residence of the President of the
Republic since 1897. Marie-
Antoinette wiled away long years
of her life in the vast château,
which she dubbed 'La Crapaudière'
('the toadhole'). To console her
and remind her of the Trianon,
Louis XVI had a dairy built in
the grounds.

The Louvre pyramid (*overleaf*)
was designed by the Sino-
American architect Ieoh Ming
Pei and was officially opened
on 30 March 1989.

ANY HISTORY OF VERSAILLES would have to begin with telling the story of Vaux-le-Vicomte. It was built at vast expense, between 1657 and 1661, by Nicolas Fouquet, finance minister to Louis XIV. Louis Le Vau drew up the plans, Charles Le Brun was responsible for the decoration and André Le Nôtre laid out the gardens. Eighteen hundred workmen laboured continuously. In 1659, La Fontaine was commissioned by Fouquet to start work on a long poem in praise of the wonders of his estate: 'In a region of these remote waters is a place named Vaux, the glory of the Universe. Its name is already abroad in a hundred different climes: Oronte is building a magnificent palace there.' Fouquet's sole lapse of taste lay in failing to predict the reaction of Louis XIV at the sight of such magnificence. When the work was finally complete, the minister organized a fantastic reception for the king. The gardens echoed with the sound of more than a thousand cascades and fountains. After various entertainments, Vatel's banquet was followed by a performance of Molière's comedy-ballet *Les Fâcheux*. Louis was mortified by this display of luxury, eclipsing that of the court; nor was he best pleased by Fouquet's motto: *Quo non ascendet* ('How high will he not go'). A few days later, the king threw his impudent servant in prison. He then ordered the construction of an even more beautiful and majestic replica of Vaux-le-Vicomte at Versailles.

Normandy

YONVILLE-L'ABBAYE (so called from an old Capuchin abbey of which not even the ruins remain) is a market-town twenty-four miles from Rouen, between the Abbeville and Beauvais roads, at the foot of a valley watered by the Rieule, a little river that runs into the Andelle after turning three water-mills near its mouth, where there are a few trout that the lads amuse themselves by fishing for on Sundays.

We leave the highroad at La Boissière and keep straight on to the top of the Leux hill, whence the valley is seen. The river that runs through it makes of it, as it were, two regions with distinct physiognomies – all on the left is pasture land, all on the right arable. The meadow stretches under a bulge of low hills to join at the back with the pasture land of the Bray country, while on the eastern side, the plain, gently rising, broadens out, showing as far as eye can follow its blond cornfields. The water, flowing by the grass, divides with a white line the colour of the roads and of the plains, and the country is like a great unfolded mantle with a green velvet cape bordered with a fringe of silver.

Before us, on the verge of the horizon, lie the oaks of the forest of Argueil, with the steeps of the Saint-Jean hills scarred from top to bottom with red irregular lines; they are rain-tracks, and these brick-tones standing out in narrow streaks against the grey colour of the mountain are due to the quantity of iron springs that flow beyond in the neighbouring country.

Here we are on the confines of Normandy, Picardy, and the Île-de-France, a bastard land, whose language is without accent as its landscape is without character. It is there that they make the worst Neufchâtel cheeses of all the arrondissement; and, on the other hand, farming is costly because so much manure is needed to enrich this friable soil full of sand and flints.

Up to 1835 there was no practicable road for getting to Yonville, but about this time a cross-road was made which joins that of Abbeville to that of Amiens, and is occasionally used by the Rouen waggoners on their way to Flanders. Yonville-l'Abbaye has remained stationary in spite of its 'new outlet'. Instead of improving the soil, they persist in keeping up the pasture lands, however depreciated they may be in value, and the lazy borough, growing away from the plain, has naturally spread riverwards. It is seen from afar sprawling along the banks like a cowherd taking a siesta by the water-side.

At the foot of the hill beyond the bridge begins a roadway, planted with young aspens, that leads in a straight line to the first houses in the place. These, fenced in by hedges, are in the middle of courtyards full of straggling buildings, wine-presses, cart-sheds, and distilleries scattered under thick trees, with ladders, poles, or scythes hung on to the branches. The thatched roofs, like fur caps drawn over eyes, reach down over about a third of the low windows, whose coarse convex glasses have knots in the middle like the bottoms of bottles. Against the plaster wall, diagonally crossed by black joists, a meagre pear-tree sometimes leans, and the ground-floors have at their door a small swing-gate, to keep out the chicks that come pilfering crumbs of bread steeped in cider on the threshold. But the courtyards grow narrower, the houses closer together, and the fences disappear; a bundle of ferns swings under a window from the end of a broomstick; there is a blacksmith's forge and then a wheelwright's, with two or three new carts outside that partly block up the way. Then across an open space appears a white house beyond a grass mound ornamented by a Cupid, his finger on his lips; two brass vases are at each end of a flight of steps; scutcheons blaze upon the door. It is the notary's house, and the finest in the place.

The church is on the other side of the street, twenty paces farther down, at the entrance of the square. The little cemetery that surrounds it, closed in by a wall breast-high, is so full of graves that the old stones, level with the ground, form a continuous pavement, on which the grass of itself has marked out regular green squares. The church was rebuilt during the last years of the reign of Charles X. The wooden roof is beginning to rot from the top, and here and there has black hollows in its blue colour. Over the door, where the organ should be, is a loft for the men, with a spiral staircase that reverberates under their wooden shoes.

Gustave Flaubert,
Madame Bovary: Provincial Manners

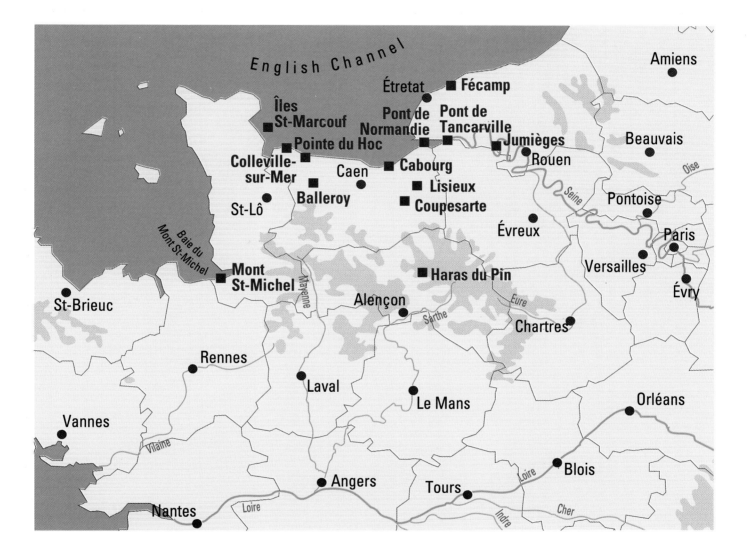

English Channel

Amiens

Étretat

Fécamp

Îles
St-Marcouf

Pont de
Normandie

Pont de
Tancarville

Beauvais

Pointe du Hoc

Jumièges

Colleville-
sur-Mer

Cabourg

Rouen

Oise

Caen

Lisieux

Pontoise

Balleroy

Coupesarte

St-Lô

Seine

Paris

Baie du
Mont-St-Michel

Évreux

Versailles

Mont
St-Michel

Haras du Pin

Évry

St-Brieuc

Mayenne

Alençon

Eure

Sarthe

Chartres

Rennes

Laval

Le Mans

Orléans

Vannes

Vilaine

Loire

Blois

Angers

Tours

Loire

Indre

Cher

Nantes

Loire

Pont-l'Évêque, Livarot, Camembert: everywhere from Cabourg to Lisieux, the cheese-making villages of the Auge Valley greet you with enticing aromas. This glorious region of France is a haven for gourmets, a setting for luxury gastronomic tours – you can, for example, sing your way along the cider route (preferably on foot). What could be better than to amble through sunken lanes, with apple trees and languid little waterways on either side, skirting old half-timbered farms? You can take a detour to see the elegant manor houses of Moutiers-Hubert, Bellou and Mont de la Vigne, or the châteaux of Le Mesnil-Guillaume, Saint-Germain-de-Livet, La Roque-Baigoult and Coupesarte (*above*). The memory of Chateaubriand still lives on at Fervaques. At Lisores you will discover a true curiosity, the delightful Fernand-Léger museum at the farm of La Bougonnières.

Just as the guide books maintain, Normandy is a land of contrasts. True, rain is a common factor, but otherwise, what could be more different than the woods and forests of the Auge Valley, the desolate wastes of Lessay that were Barbey d'Aurevilly's inspiration, the Proustian seaside resorts, the cliffs at Étretat or the marshy plains of the lower Seine Valley? How is it they ever came to form a single region? The answer, of course, lies with the Northmen, or Normans, who under the Vikings occupied the area in successive waves from the tenth century onwards; it still bears the marks of their violence.

One of France's finest ruins, the abbey of Jumièges (*left*) was founded by Saint Philibert in 654 AD, sacked by the Vikings and then restored by the Benedictines. In the Revolution it suffered the further indignity of being put up for public auction.

'In the all-devouring silence – for its sands also suck in sound, except the thunder – the Mount appears at its most eloquent, just as its intricate detail appears to best effect against this abundant simplicity, and so too its colour, all its riches.' This is how Jean de La Varende described the Mont Saint-Michel. According to legend, its polders cover the submerged forest of Scissy. In the eighth century, the archangel Michael prompted Auber, Bishop of Avranches, to build an oratory on the Mount. Since then, one building has been erected on top of another – Carolingian, Gothic, Roman – and, in 1897, it was crowned with a forty-metre spire. The island has always been threatened by natural disasters, shifting sands and tides. A variety of precautionary measures have up till now prevented it from foundering. A bridge is shortly to replace the solid causeway that provides the approach route, it being the major cause of silting in the bay. The formidable Mont Saint-Michel was the symbol of resistance during the Hundred Years War. It must now withstand an influx of tourism.

THE PONT DE TANCARVILLE (*left*) – 1,410 metres long and 125 metres high – spans the Seine estuary. Erected in 1958, it has rapidly acquired the status of a national treasure, guaranteed to make the passing foreign visitor pause in envious admiration. The Pont de Normandie (*above*) has a central span of 856 metres. Built to relieve pressure on the Pont de Tancarville, this enormous structure, opened in January 1995, lies even closer to the mouth of the Seine. It is equipped with 184 cables supporting the weight of the roadway and is capable of resisting winds gusting at over 200 miles an hour. A marvel of recent technology, it is the most advanced bridge of its kind in the world, although the Tarata bridge in Japan is due to be opened at the end of the century.

ON 5 JUNE 1944, the Normandy beaches were preparing for D-Day. The people of Colleville, Sainte-Mère-Église, Arromanches and Luc-sur-Mer awaited liberation with typical Norman stoicism. At nine o'clock in the evening the first boats appeared over the horizon off the Normandy shore. The noise of aircraft could be heard. The Allied offensive, known as Operation Overlord, began at a quarter past midnight. American airborne divisions and hundreds of parachutists landed in the canton of Sainte-Mère-Église. By half past four the flag was flying over the town and the naval disembarkation was about to start. It was an apocalyptic attack. The 9,386 white marble crosses in the American cemetery (*opposite*) outside Colleville-Saint-Laurent are a reminder of the thousands of American soldiers who lost their lives in the fighting. The bomb damage was such that the Normans were obliged to rebuild many major towns, among them Caen and Le Havre. Lisieux (*above*), in the department of Calvados, lost most of its attractive half-timbered houses. The cathedral of Saint-Pierre (late twelfth–early thirteenth century) was spared, as was the Musée du Vieux-Lisieux and the Chapelle du Carmel, which houses the relics of Saint Theresa.

In 1665, Colbert set up publicly owned stud farms for breeding horses. They were closed down during the Revolution but restored to their former glory in the late nineteenth century. The Haras du Pin (*above*) remains one of the best known. The plans for this 'Versailles for horses' were drawn up by Jules Hardouin-Mansart and André Le Nôtre. It was François Mansart – not to be confused with Jules – who built the château of Balleroy (*opposite*), the decoration of which was undertaken once again by Le Nôtre. The owner was Jean de Choisy, chancellor to Gaston d'Orléans. For three centuries the building was passed down to the marquesses of Balleroy and it then became the property of the American aviator Malcolm Forbes. The interior of the château has an impressive portrait gallery and wall hangings identical to those in the Grand Trianon, Versailles. Of particular interest, however, are the former stables, now converted into a museum of hot-air and gas balloons – a fact that has to be mentioned in a volume devoted to aerial photography. Our present-day techniques owe much to those who copied the example of the Montgolfier brothers – they invented the first hot-air balloon, which made its ascent in 1783. In 1857, Nadar (whose real name was Félix Tournachon) took his first lessons in aerostatics using a machine designed by the Godard brothers, an illustrious family of balloonists. From the basket of their balloon, he carried out his first experiments in aerial photography, so giving the initial impetus to what was to prove a highly popular genre.

The fort built by Napoleon (*preceding pages*) on the Îles Saint-Marcouf, off Cotentin.

MYSTERY SURROUNDS THE LIFE of Guy de Maupassant, even his birth: according to the register, he was born on 5 August 1850 at Tourville-sur-Arques in the magnificent château of Miromesnil, which his family had rented for the summer. In fact, today it is generally accepted that Laure de Maupassant gave birth at Fécamp (*preceding pages*) in the little rue Sous-le-Bois, now known as the Quai Guy-de-Maupassant, which is an infinitely less fashionable address. It is interesting that pure snobbery can lead to the falsification of an official document, and that one small detail can bring in its wake a whole series of legends – among them, that the parents were trying to disguise the child's doubtful paternity and that Maupassant was the natural son of Gustave Flaubert. ... Whatever the truth, Laure and Gustave de Maupassant should not have despised Fécamp. In the seventh century, the relic of the *precieux-sang* was deposited in a monastery belonging to the town. Duke Richard I ordered the rebuilding of a magnificent church dedicated to the Holy Trinity. In the eleventh century, until the rise of the Mont Saint-Michel, Fécamp was the principal centre of pilgrimage in Normandy. Duke Richard's church burned down after it was hit by a thunderbolt, and was rebuilt in the twelfth and thirteen centuries. The Pointe du Hoc (*left*) was devastated by the landing operations during the Allied invasion. To take out a German battery stationed on the cape, the American commander subjected it to continuous bombardment. Then on the morning of 6 June 1944, the second batallion of Rangers stormed it after scaling the cliffs with ropes, ladders and grappling hooks, at the cost of many lives. A granite obelisk commemorates these heroic engagements.

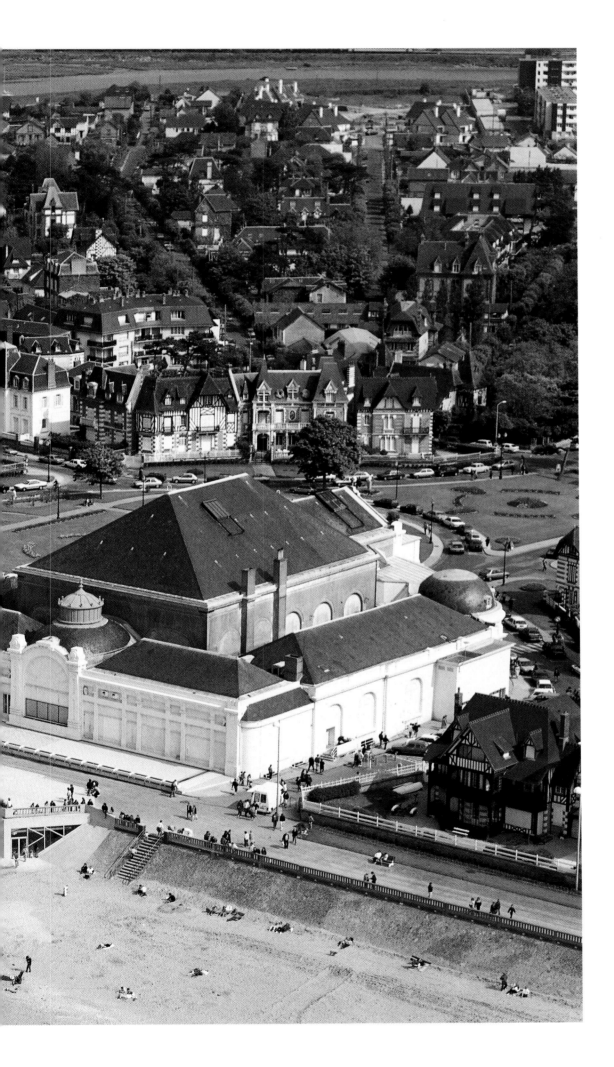

MARCEL PROUST'S SETTING FOR *À la recherche du temps perdu* was inspired by the Normandy coast – his walks along the broad beaches of Cabourg to Deauville or Honfleur. At Cabourg (*left*), which Proust called Balbec in his book, he stayed at the Grand Hôtel in 1891 and again between 1907 and 1914. Today, the resort has not changed, the atmosphere is still one of old-fashioned luxury. Proust used to spend his days in bed in his room, writing, and would then go downstairs with his head swathed in black veiling, and linger over a canapé, lost in thought, before proceeding as was sometimes his wont to the large dining room. At night, in the light, 'this became like an immense and wonderful aquarium in front of whose glass wall the working population of Balbec, the fishermen and also the tradesmen's families, invisible in the dark, pressed against the pane to glimpse these people's luxurious life floating gently past on golden eddies, as extraordinary to the poor as the life of strange fish and molluscs' (*À l'ombre des jeunes filles en fleurs*).

The Loire

Valley

So one Thursday morning I left Tours by the Saint-Eloy gate, I crossed the bridges of Saint-Sauveur, I reached Poncher, my nose in the air in front of every house I passed, and was on the road to Chinon. For the first time in my life I could rest under a tree, walk fast or slowly as I list, without being called to account by any one. To a poor creature so utterly crushed by the various despotisms which weigh more or less on every young life, the first taste of freedom, though exerted in trifles, brought unspeakable expansion to my soul.

Several reasons combined to make that a high day full of delights. In my childhood my walks had never taken me more than a league out of the town. My excursions in the neighbourhood of Pont-le-Voy and the walks I had taken in Paris had not surfeited me with rural beauty. Nevertheless, I had retained from the earliest impressions of my life a strong feeling of the beauty inherent in the scenery round Tours, with which I was familiar. Thus, though I was new to what constitutes the poetry of a site, I was unconsciously exacting, as men are who have conceived of the ideal of an art without ever having practised it.

To go to the château of Frapesle, those who walk or ride shorten the way by crossing the common known as the Landes de Charlemagne, a waste lying at the top of the plateau which divides the valley of the Cher from that of the Indre, and which is reached by a cross-road from Champy. This flat and sandy down, depressing enough for about a league, ends in a coppice adjoining the road to Saché, the village nearest to Frapesle. This country lane, leading into the Chinon road at some distance beyond Ballan, skirts an undulating plain devoid of remarkable features as far as the hamlet of Artanne. Thence a valley opens down to the Loire, from Montvazon at the head; the hills seem to rebound under the country-houses on each range of slopes; it is a glorious emerald basin, and at the bottom the Indre winds in serpentine curves. I was startled by the view into a rapturous astonishment for which the dulness of the Landes or the fatigue of my walk had prepared me: If this woman, the flower of her sex, inhabits a spot on earth, it must be this!

At the thought I leaned against a walnut tree; and now, whenever I revisit that beloved valley, I go to rest under its boughs. Under that tree, the confidant of all my thoughts, I examine myself as to the changes that may have taken place during the time that has elapsed since last I left it.

My heart had not deceived me: it was there that she dwelt; the first château I could see on a shelf of the down was her home. When I sat down under my walnut-tree, the noonday sun struck sparks from the slates of *her* roof and the glass panes of *her* windows. Her cambric dress was the white spot I could see among some vines under a pleached alley. She was, as you know already, though as yet you know nothing, the Lily of this Valley, where she grew for heaven, filling it with the fragrance of her virtues. I saw an emblem of infinite love with nothing to keep it alive but an object only once seen, in the long watery ribband which glistens in the sun between two green banks, in the rows of poplars which deck that vale of love with moving tracery, in the oak woods thrust forward between the vineyards on the hillsides rounded by the river into constant variety, and in the soft outlines crossing each other and fading to the horizon.

If you wish to see Nature fair and virginal as a bride, go thither some spring day; if you want to solace the bleeding wounds of your heart, return in the late days of autumn. In spring Love flutters his wings under the open sky; in autumn we dream of those who are no more. Weak lungs inhale a healing freshness, the eye finds rest on golden-hued groves from which the soul borrows sweet peace.

At the moment when I looked down on the valley of the Indre, the mills on its falls gave voice to the murmuring vale; the poplars laughed as they swayed; there was not a cloud in the sky; the birds sang, the grasshoppers chirped, everything was melody. Never ask me again why I love Touraine? I do not love it as we love our childhood's home, nor as we love an oasis in the desert; I love it as an artist loves art. I love it less than I love you; still, but for Touraine, perhaps I should not now be alive.

Without knowing why, my eyes were riveted to the white spot, to the woman who shone in that garden as the bell of a convolvulus shines among shrubs and is blighted by a touch. My soul deeply stirred, I went down into this bower, and presently saw a village, which to my highly strung poetic mood seemed matchless.

Honoré de Balzac, *The Lily of the Valley*

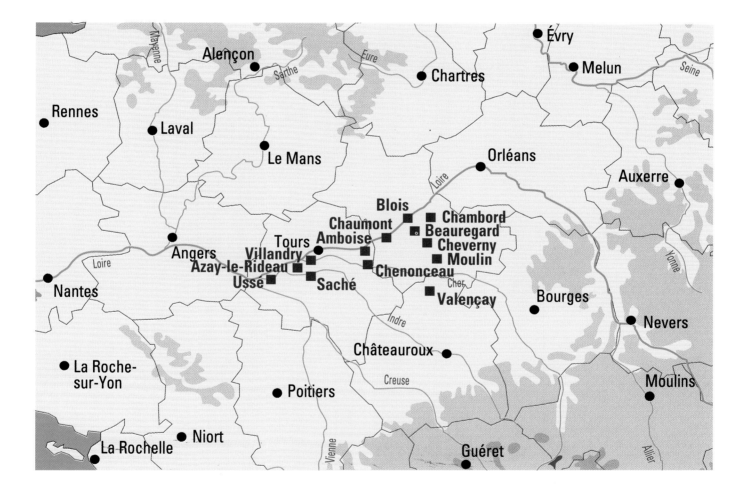

'IT IS THE LAND OF *laughter* and *leisure*. As brightly green in August as it is in May, full of fruit and trees. If you look across from the river's edge, the other bank seems suspended in the air, so faithfully does the water reflect the sky: the sand at the bottom, then the willow lapping the water; behind that, the poplar, the aspen, the walnut, islands receding among

and court came down from their heights to pose on river banks or occupy the centre stage in their gardens. Keeps, moats and towers of any sort were henceforth purely decorative. Boccaccio's stories came from Italy, along with paintings and other works of art. A team of poets celebrated the region and all its delights. Ladies-in-waiting were treated like queens – François I

other islands; and higher still, the rounded tops of trees rippling gently into the distance, one against the other.' That is how Jules Michelet described the Loire, 'that soft and sensual land', in his *Tableau de la France*. The Renaissance shaped its landscape and refined its way of life. Under the Valois, the castles abandoned any defensive role and became instead theatres in which royalty could disport itself. King

showered them with costly trinkets and threatened to hang anyone who showed them disrespect. Hardly surprising that Charles Perrault sought the inspiration for his fairy-tales in the Loire valley. The fifteenth-century château of Ussé (*left*) is said to have been his model for *The Sleeping Beauty*.

Cheverny (*above*) is a seventeenth-century masterpiece on the borders of the Sologne.

For lovers of ancient buildings, the peaceful Loire valley offers a cornucopia of noble edifices. The château of Beauregard (*above*) is still a jewel of Renaissance style, despite alterations. The château of Amboise (*opposite*) has fortifications that date from the Romano-Gallic period. Charles VIII had it extended to make it 'an earthly paradise' commensurate with his love of Italianate ostentation. He died there, in 1498, having banged his head against a low doorway leading into a gallery. Under François I, extravagance reached its apogee at Amboise, with festivities, tournaments, fights with wild animals, and also charming ballets performed by young women. But the châteaux did not only provide entertainment: the conspiracy of Amboise in 1560, led by the Huguenot La Renaudie, ended in a bloodbath. The conspirators were hanged, drowned in the Loire, beheaded or drawn and quartered. Today, Amboise is a peaceful place, its past splendours evoked in spectacles of *son et lumière*.

The Loire at Blois (*preceeding pages*).

'CHAMBORD IS THE EPITOME of human achievement,' exclaimed the Holy Roman Emperor Charles V. Alfred de Vigny called it the 'magic château'. Apparently, we owe the design of this vast and extravagant building to the talents of Leonardo da Vinci. François I had installed the great painter at the manor of Clos-Lucé, near Amboise, in 1516, but he died three years later as work was getting under way. The king spent a fortune on Chambord, and yet at the time of his death in 1547 it was still not finished – and nor was it when his son Henri II died in 1559. In the seventeenth century, Chambord, by then owned by the comté of Blois, reverted to Louis XIV. He stayed there nine times and undertook major renovations. Molière and Lulli first performed *Monsieur de Pourceaugnac* and later *Le Bourgeois gentilhomme* there. They would go to almost any length to obtain a smile from the king. And when they did succeed and he deigned to show amusement, then all the court would split their sides laughing.

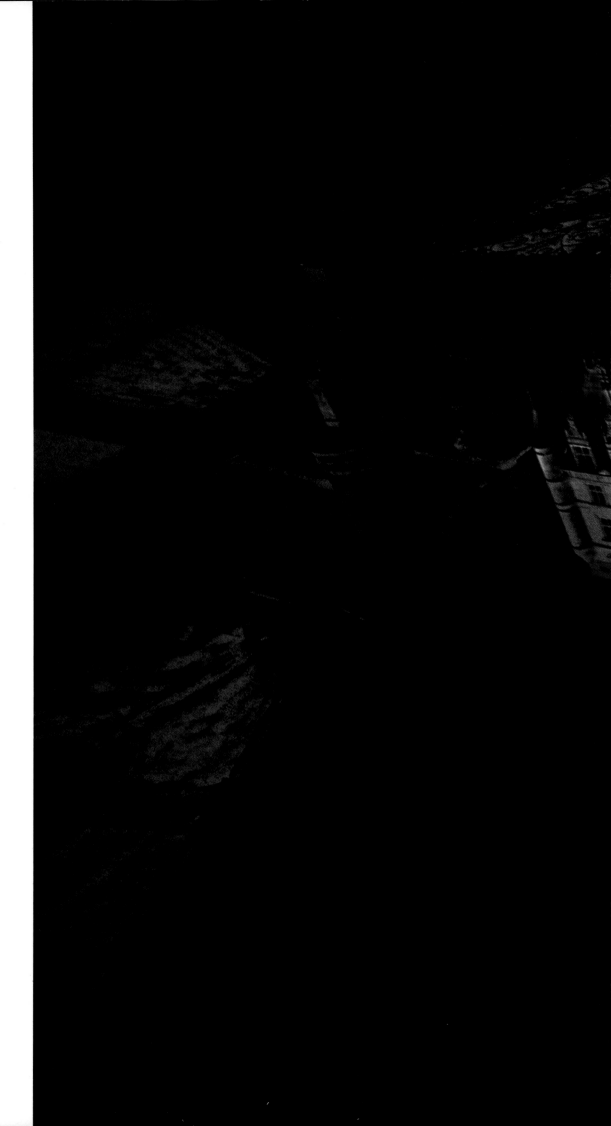

CHENONCEAU'S SUPERB ARCHES
span the River Cher. Elegant
architecture, harmonious
proportions, magnificent
furnishings ... will there ever be
enough adjectives to do justice to
Chenonceau? The château dates
from the sixteenth century –
Henri II gave it as a gift to his
favourite, the palely beautiful
Diane de Poitiers, who was twenty
years his junior. At the king's death
in 1559, his abandoned queen,
Catherine de Médicis, forced her
rival to give her Chenonceau in
exchange for Chaumont. The regent
lived in great style in her new home
– there were masquerades with
sirens, nymphs and satyrs, festivals,
fireworks and naval battles. In the
eighteenth century, Chenonceau
passed to the wealthy farmer
Dupin, whose wife presided over
a famous salon. She engaged Jean-
Jacques Rousseau as private tutor
for her appallingly spoilt young
son. He thoroughly enjoyed his
time at Chenonceau, put on vast
amounts of weight and rapidly
gave up teaching and instead
wrote *Émile ou de l'éducation*.

BUILT ON THE HIGHEST hilltop on the banks of the Loire, it encloses the broad summit inside its tall outer walls and giant towers; high slate bell-towers carry the eye upwards, giving the building that look of a monastery, that religious air of all our old châteaux,' wrote Alfred de Vigny of Chaumont-sur-Loire (*opposite*). This former tenth-century manor house belonged to the Amboise family for five hundred years. It was then acquired by Catherine de Médicis, who installed her personal astrologer, the mysterious Florentine Cosimo Ruggieri, before forcing Diane de Poitiers to take the château in exchange for Chenonceau. Diane de Poitiers set about various works but these were cut short by her death in 1566. Notable among the many subsequent occupants is Madame de Staël, who took refuge there in 1810 when Napoleon's wrath obliged her to leave Paris. She moved in her own 'court', among them Benjamin Constant and Madame Récamier. The Princesse de Broglie, who bought the château in 1875, also left her mark, although largely with a programme of restoration and the construction of sumptuously appointed annexes. At present Chaumont is owned by the state and appears to be somewhat dilapidated, the splendid receptions that echoed within its walls during the Belle Époque are now ancient history. The fine château of Le Moulin (*above*), near Lassay-sur-Croisne, was built by Philippe du Moulin, between 1480 and 1506.

The château of Valençay (*overleaf*) was built in the sixteenth century by Jacques d'Étampes.

'A MANY-FACETED DIAMOND, set off by the Indre, mounted on layers covered with flowers,' wrote Balzac of Azay-le-Rideau. This Renaissance château (*left and opposite*), built by the financier Gilles Berthelot, exemplifies the transition from the castle as fortress to the castle as gracious dwelling. Italianate influences are combined with elements of medieval architecture, but the towers, machicolations and moats are already purely ornamental. The château does not have the eventful history of Chenonceau – with which it has certain affinities – or of Blois, to which it was once subject; and yet it is one of the most famous and admired of all the châteaux in the Loire. Four miles from Azay is the château of Saché, formerly owned by a Monsieur de Margonne, a friend of Balzac and his mother's former lover. The writer, although born in Tours in 1799, spent very little time in the area. In a sense one could say that he rediscovered his roots through Saché, which provided him with a haven away from the city and his creditors – this did not, however, stop him working non-stop from two in the morning through till the evening. He wrote several novels there, among them *Le Lys dans la vallée*.

The château of Villandry and its celebrated gardens (*overleaf*).

Brittany

and la Vendée

IT HAS BEEN SAID that Paris, Rouen and Le Havre are one town and the Seine is its high street. Strike out to the south of this magnificent road, where château follows château, village follows village; go from Seine-Inférieure to Calvados, and from Calvados on to the Channel, and rich and fertile though the land may be, the towns diminish in number, and so do the arable fields; the grazing pastures increase. Already an austere place, it will become wild and desolate. The lofty châteaux of Normandy will be replaced by the low manor houses of Brittany. The costumes seem to echo the changes in the architecture. The triumphal bonnet of the women of Caux aptly distinguishes the daughters of England's conquerors; as you approach Caen, it widens out; from Villedieu on, it becomes flatter; in Saint-Malo, it divides and flies in the wind, sometimes like the sails of a windmill, sometimes the sails of a boat. Leather clothes, to take another example, begin in Laval. The increasingly impenetrable forests, the solitude of La Trappe, where the monks share their reclusive life, the evocative names of the towns, Fougères and Rennes ('Rennes' can mean the same as 'fougère', i.e. 'bracken'), the grey waters of the Mayenne and the Vilaine are all indicative of this rugged land.

All the same, it is here we mean to start our study of France. As the eldest daughter of the monarchy, it is the province of the Celts that must take precedence. ...

Poor, hard Brittany, France's element of resistance, its fields of quartz and schist extend from the slate quarries of Châteaulin, near Brest, to the slate quarries of Angers. That is the extent of its geological range, although, from Angers to Rennes there is a disputed and shifting area, like the border between England and Scotland, which early on escaped from Breton control. The Breton language does not even start in Rennes but nearer Elven, Pontivy, Loudéac and Châtelaudren. From here to the Pointe du Finistère is the real Britanny, Breton-speaking Brittany, a land that has become entirely foreign to ours for the simple reason that it has remained too loyal to our original traditions; so Gallic that it is very little French; and it would have escaped us altogether on more than one occasion if we did not have it held tight, as if with pincers and tongs, between four French towns of strong and rugged character: Nantes and Saint-Malo, Rennes and Brest.

And yet this poor old province has saved us more than once; often when our country had its back to the wall and was near despair, there were Breton chests and Breton heads harder than any foreign sword. When the Norsemen overran our coasts and rivers with impunity, it was the Breton Noménoé who started the resistance; the English were repelled in the fourteenth century by Duguesclin, and in the seventeenth by Richemont; in the eighteenth, they were hounded across the seas by Duguay-Trouin. No war of religious or political freedom boasts any hero more innocent and more pure than Lanoue or Latour d'Auvergne, the first Republican grenadier. He came from Nantes, if tradition is to be believed, and uttered the last cry of Waterloo: the guard dies and does not surrender! ...

At its two gateways, Brittany has two forests, the woodlands of Normandy and of La Vendée; two towns, Saint-Malo and Nantes, the town of the privateers and that of the slave-traders. Saint-Malo has a singularly ugly and sinister appearance; and in addition, something quite mysterious that is encountered continuously throughout the peninsula, in the costumes, pictures and monuments. A small rich town, dark and desolate, a nest of vultures and sea-eagles, sometimes an island, sometimes a peninsula, depending on the ebb and flow of the tide; edged all about with dirty, fetid reefs where the seaweed rots to high heaven. Extending into the distance, a coast of white jagged rocks, sharp as razors. War is a good time for Saint-Malo; they know no more delightful occasion for celebration. ... When recently there was a prospect of rushing the Dutch ships, you should have seen them on their black walls with their spy-glasses, already scouring every part of the ocean.

At the other end is Brest, the great military port, Richelieu's idea, Louis XIV's implementation: fort, arsenal and convict prison, cannons, vessels, armies, France's might piled high at the opposite end of the country: and all that in an enclosed harbour, where you suffocate between two mountains covered in massive buildings.

Jules Michelet, *Tableau de la France*

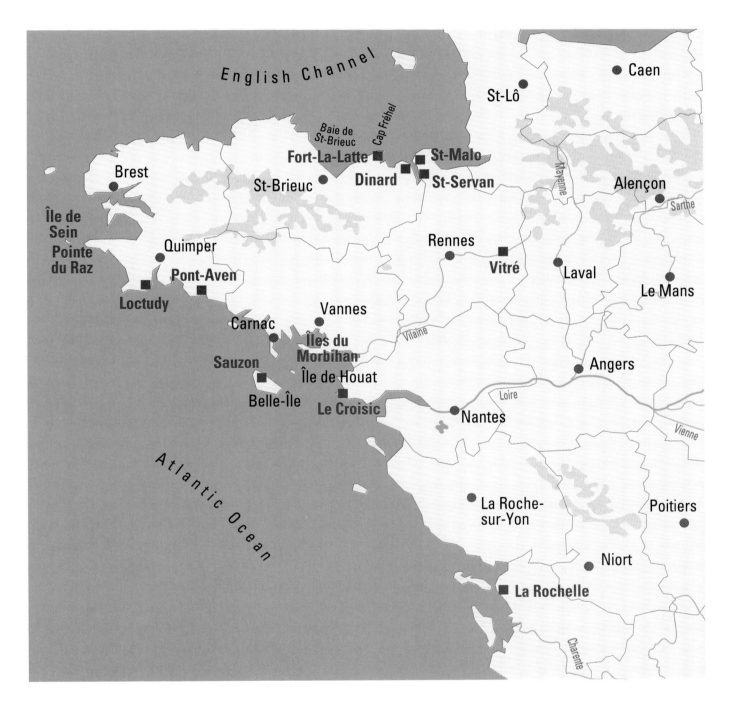

English Channel

Caen

St-Lô

Baie de
St-Brieuc

Cap Fréhel

Fort-La-Latte

St-Malo

Dinard

St-Servan

Brest

Mayenne

Alençon

Sarthe

St-Brieuc

Île de
Sein

Pointe
du Raz

Quimper

Rennes

Vitré

Laval

Le Mans

Pont-Aven

Loctudy

Vannes

Carnac

Îles du
Morbihan

Vilaine

Sauzon

Île de Houat

Angers

Loire

Belle-Île

Le Croisic

Nantes

Vienne

Atlantic Ocean

La Roche-
sur-Yon

Poitiers

Niort

La Rochelle

Charente

THE ROCKY EXTREMITY of ancient Cornouaille, the Pointe du Raz (*left*), is a popular tourist destination, despite a sometimes dangerous swell and treacherous whirlpools like the Enfer de Plogoff. It is a place of legends. Some believe that just offshore lies the site of the submerged town of Is (although others place it in the Baie de Douarnenez). Two miles to the north-east is the delightfully

the *Ankou* is death, the traditional figure of a skeleton carrying a scythe, the one who comes to carry you off to the next world. Among the many Breton cults, that of the departed souls holds pride of place. 'Undoubtedly we are the heirs of the Celts,' wrote Pierre Jakez Hélias. 'For us death is a funereal celebration marking the departure of a person to another world that exists alongside this one.'

named 'Baie des Trépassés' or 'bay of departed souls' from where it is said a group of Druids who were shipwrecked off the Île de Sein embarked. At dusk you may catch sight of a boat in full sail, with no crew aboard save a solitary figure at the helm. This is the *Ankou*, whose name sends a shiver through all Bretons. For

Dinard (*above*) is on the Rance estuary. Early this century, the English gentry transformed what was once a small fishing port into an attractive Breton Riviera – hence these extraordinary neo-Gothic residences, permanent reminders of the ancestral ties between this region and the Anglo-Saxon countries.

THE CASTLE, rebuilt in the fourteenth and fifteenth centuries, complete with drawbridge and machicolated towers, looks down over a Gothic town full of ancient charm – time seems to stand still in Vitré. In the old town you must visit the rue Baudrairie, formerly the quarter occupied by the *baudroyeurs* or leatherworkers who gave the street its name. Each house has a porch and wooden timbering, a mark of the prosperity achieved through trade – between the fifteenth and the eighteenth century, Vitré's reputation extended throughout Europe and even to America and India, because of the sheets, canvas and leather it produced. As you continue to walk through the Breton city's maze of streets, you come to the rue Sévigné, where the famous Madame de Sévigné stayed in the seventeenth century. Admirers of this distinguished woman of letters could even make a short literary pilgrimage to visit the château of Rochers-Sévigné, four miles from Vitré. You get there through woodland and it is not unattractive. The house itself is a fifteenth-century building remodelled in the sixteenth century, square in form with an octagonal tower. Madame de Sévigné faced financial ruin after her husband was killed in a duel in 1651, and spent long periods there, writing in all 267 letters to her daughter. The extensive park has flower beds which were laid out by Le Nôtre at the end of the seventeenth century, and is equally worthy of note. The marquise gave each avenue an attractive and unusual name: 'The Solitary', 'The Holy Terror', 'The Royal' and even 'My Mother's Mood'.

CÔTES-DU-NORD, Finistère, Ille-et-Vilaine, Loire-Atlantique, Morbihan (*above*): Brittany owes its present composition to the Revolution (in which the Club Breton, later the Club des Jacobins, played such a central role). During this period the seigniorial fiefdoms disappeared, and with them their associated 'liberties and exemptions'. But the former Armorica ('land of the sea') remains even today a province with a separate life of its own, its own language – the subject of many battles – its own traditions, saints, religious festivals, its own myths and legendary exploits. The

Tour Solidor (*opposite*) at Saint-Servan-sur-Mer, dominating the Rance estuary, houses a museum dedicated to the great Breton epic of the voyage around Cape Horn. There is an outstanding collection of books, prints and model ships, among them one of the *Victoria*, the first craft to circumnavigate the globe, in 1,084 days, between 1519 and 1522. On the three storeys of this sixteenth-century tower, restored in the seventeenth century, there are memorabilia and objects of all kinds evoking the harsh and perilous life of the sailors who braved the storms of Cape Horn.

'SAINT-MALO, built on the sea and ringed by ramparts, appears at first sight like a crown of stones set down on the waves, its battlements the flowerets' (Flaubert, *Par les champs et par les grèves*). In the spring of 1847, Gustave Flaubert, aged twenty-five, set out for Brittany with his staunch friend Maxime Du Camp. 'Alone, independent, together!', they were in flight from civilization and overprotective mothers. The young men, notebooks in pockets – the purpose of the trip was also to produce a collaborative book – were eager to soak up every new experience. This is exactly the sort of openminded and enthusiastic attitude in which journeys should be undertaken. Brittany – 'land's end' – lends itself perfectly to such an adventure. Saint-Malo (*left*), an old pirate stronghold, remains an ideal staging-post. It was from here that the navigator Jacques Cartier set out in 1534 to explore the St Lawrence in Canada. As well as the ramparts, the Place Chateaubriand is worth a visit, for it was here that the great writer was born. In the same square is the fifteenth-century castle that houses the local museum.

The Côte de Lumière (*above*) in la Vendée is characterized by flat islands and quiet woodlands.

PONT-AVEN (*opposite*), in the district of Cornouailles, owes its fame to the artists who made it their home. Between 1886 and 1889, before Gauguin set sail for Tahiti, he stayed there on three occasions. Drawing in his wake a bevy of young painters, among them Émile Bernard and Paul Sérusier, he came to be viewed as the leader of the Pont-Aven school. The artists caused considerable havoc in the Breton community, with their drunkenness, brawls, debts and so forth. It was not unheard of to see red-painted geese tottering drunkenly through the streets. Today, this is all part of local folklore, as is the name of Théodore Botrel, immortal author of *La Paimpolaise*, an inhabitant of the town since 1912. On the first Sunday in August, the women don traditional dress for the festival of Les Fleurs d'Ajoncs, created by the Breton bard.

Dinard (*above*) is on the Rance estuary.

LA ROCHELLE is a jewel among cities. Sacked and pillaged over the centuries, it has frequently had to defend itself from attack. The French Wars of Religion, sieges, famines and repression have served only to harden this fierce town's determination to resist. Evidence of this is supplied by the fortifications of the old harbour, its entrance guarded by the Tour Saint-Nicolas and Tour de la Chaîne, both built in the fourteenth century. To the right of the entrance is the Tour de la Lanterne, which was constructed much later. It has a tall upper section and – as the name would suggest – a lantern, originally used as a beacon. The dignified atmosphere of the old port, its bustling life and light, have attracted the attention of painters from Joseph Vernet to Corot and the Impressionists. In a past age, wine, salt, cloth, wool, spices and cocoa all passed over its quays. Today, the town is dedicated largely to fishing and pleasure. Belle-Île-en-Mer was a no less coveted site in previous centuries, although attacked by the English and Dutch navies, it has remained French. There is much to see on this enchanting island: on the west, the Côte Sauvage and Grotte de l'Apothicaire; to the east, the small capital of Le Palais, which has within it the Citadelle Vauban, as well as Sauzon (*preceding pages*), an attractive harbour resort often called the 'port fleuri'; then, to the north, the Pointe des Poulains. There, beside an inlet, is the small fort in which Sarah Bernhardt chose to spend her vacations, far from the madding crowd.

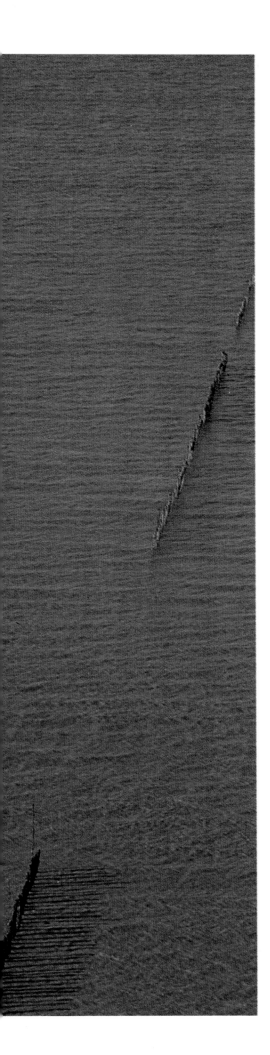

Out to sea from the Pointe du Raz lies the small Île de Sein (*top*), to which Saint Guénolé brought the gospel in the fifth century. Many legends surround the island, which is often cut off from the mainland by gales – it may be the *insula Sena* referred to by the Romans, or the island of the nine prophetesses of the navigators, that of the Seven Slumbers, or of the Souls of the Departed. The Senans have a reputation for bravery and tenacity. Bretons to the last, they defy the tidal waves that have on occasion been known to swamp the island. The Senans were also the first members of the French Resistance. When the call went out, on 18 June 1940, all the men on the island, some 150 sailors in all, crossed over the Channel in fishing boats to join forces with the Free French. General de Gaulle later remembered their courage and exempted the islanders from paying taxes. With oysters, shellfish, sardines, crabs and lobsters all at their disposal, the Croisicais, as the fortunate inhabitants of Le Croisic in Loire-Atlantique (*left*) are known, along with the Senans derive their living mainly from exploitation of the sea. The same is true of Loctudy (*above*), a little fishing village and seaside resort at the mouth of the Pont-l'Abbé River, in the heart of the old Pays Bigouden.

Aquitaine

and the Pyrenees

At Bordeaux, where he had arrived after travelling through the night, he had joined, not without emotion, the train for Irun, which runs in a direct line towards the south, through the monotony of interminable barren plains. He had taken a corner seat by the window on the right in order that he might see at the first possible moment the Bay of Biscay and the outlines of the high mountains of Spain.

Later, as he drew near to Bayonne, he was thrilled by the sight, at the level crossings, of the first Basque bonnets, of the first Basque houses amid the pines and the oak trees.

And at St Jean-de-Luz at last, as he got out of the train, he felt a little as if he were intoxicated. ... First of all, coming from the fogs and cold which had already begun in northern France, there was here the sudden and delightful impression of a warmer climate, the sensation of entering a greenhouse. The sun was shining brilliantly; the south wind, the sweet wind from the south, was blowing gently, and the Pyrenees stood out in magnificent colours against the wide, clear sky. And then women were passing, young women whose laugh had the music of the south and of Spain, young women with the elegance and easy grace of the women of his own Basque country, who, after the heavy blondes of the north, troubled him more even than all these illusions of summer. But quickly his mood changed. Of what use was it to let himself be captivated by the charm that was here, since this rediscovered country of his was for him empty for ever? How could it alter his infinite despair, this fascinating grace of the women, all this ironic cheerfulness of the sky, of men and things?

No! Let him rather seek his home, return to his village, and embrace his mother!

As he had anticipated, the diligence which runs daily to Etchezar had left two hours before. But no whit put out, he proposed to walk the long road, so familiar to him of old, so as to reach home, nevertheless, the same evening, before the night was quite dark.

He went, therefore, and bought some *espadrilles*, the footwear of his excursions of earlier years. And stepping out rapidly as became a mountaineer, with long, swinging strides, he plunged at once into the heart of the silent countryside, by roads which for him were full of memories.

November was drawing to a close, in the warm radiance of the sun which always lingers on these Pyrenean slopes. For some days now, over the Basque country, this same clear and luminous sky had prevailed, above the woods now half-leafless, above the mountains reddened with the ardent colour of the ferns. By the roadside grew tall grasses, as in the month of May, and large umbellar flowers which had mistaken the season. In the hedges, privet and eglantine were blooming again, to the buzzing of the last bees, and there fluttered about a few belated butterflies, to whom death had allowed a short reprieve of some weeks.

The Basque houses emerged here and there from the trees, very high, with overhanging roofs, very white in their extreme old age, with their shutters brown and green, an old and faded green. And everywhere, on their wooden balconies, golden yellow pumpkins were drying, and bunches of pink haricots; everywhere, on their walls, were strung, like pretty strings of coral beads, garlands of red pimentos: all the good things of the still fecund earth, all the good things of the old nourishing soil, stored thus, according to the usage of centuries, in provision for the dark months when the kindly warmth should be no more.

And after the mists of the northern autumn, this clearness of the air, this southern sunshine, every new familiar detail of the country, awakened in the complex soul of Ramuntcho infinite memories, bitter sweet.

It was the season for the cutting of the ferns which form the fleece of the red hillsides. And large bullock-wagons, laden with this harvest, were rumbling peacefully, through the clear, melancholy sunshine, towards the isolated farmhouses, leaving behind them the trail of their perfume. Very slowly, along the mountain roads, went these enormous loads of ferns; very slowly, with a tinkle of little bells. Yoked oxen, indolent and strong – coifed all with the traditional tawny-coloured sheep's-skin which gave them the appearance of bisons or aurochs – hauled these heavy wagons, the wheels of which were simple discs, similar to those of the wagons of antiquity.

Pierre Loti,
A Tale of the Pyrenees (Ramuntcho)

Bassin de
Marennes-Oléron

Charente

Limoges

Clermont-
Ferrand

Angoulême

Pauillac

Château-
Latour

Périgueux

Tulle

Aurillac

Bordeaux

Dordogne

Lot

Bassin
d'Arcachon

Atlantic Ocean

Garonne

Cahors

Aveyron

Rodez

Agen

Mt-de-Marsan

Montauban

Tarn

Midouze

Albi

Auch

St.-Jean-de-Luz

Toulouse

Pau

Tarbes

Lourdes

Garonne

Carcassonne

Foix

Quéribus

Fenouillèdes

Perpignan

Ille-sur-Têt

Eus

Têt

SPAIN

Andorra

Le Canigou

Serrabone

Cap Béar

Q UÉRIBUS, MONTSÉGUR,
Minerve, Cabaret, Puilaurens:
the sites of the so-called Cathar
châteaux, enduring reminders of
the bloody crusade in the thirteenth
century against the Albigenses –
it was in these fortresses that the
heretics hounded by the Church
mounted their last ditch resistance.
The ancient citadel of Quéribus
(*opposite*), now a ruin, sits atop
an impressive rocky spur at an
altitude of 729 metres. Its wind-
lashed vertical cliff-face dominates a
crest that marks the ancient frontier
between France and Aragon, today

the boundary between the
departments of Aude and
the Pyrénées-Orientales. This
fortress was one of the last Cathar
strongholds, its massive keep
capable of withstanding armies
of considerable size. The last rebels
managed to take refuge here before
the royal troops arrived, but they
were betrayed and ultimately
Quéribus was overwhelmed. Its fall
in 1255 marked the end of a heresy
greatly feared by the Church, and
the beginning of a significant period
of French unity. After its capture,
the citadel became a strategic

position for the defence of the plain
of Roussillon. Once impregnable,
it is today surrounded by carparks
so tourists have easy access and can
enjoy the view over Les Albères, the
Mediterranean and Le Canigou, or
the massifs of Le Puigmal and Le
Carlit. Although very little remains
of the original structure, the interior
includes a high Gothic hall, whose
unusual design and lighting have
been interpreted in a variety of
ways as indicative of some form
of solar symbolism.

Eus (*above*) is a small village
in Roussillon.

On the Côte d'Argent, where the Pyrenees meet the Atlantic, sardine fishing has long been a staple industry. Adjacent to Saint-Jean-de-Luz, and often assumed to be part of it, Ciboure lies just across the bridge. This typical Basque port was formerly settled by the Cascarots, or Spanish gypsies, and then by fishermen from the Pays Bigouden. It prides itself on the fact that Maurice Ravel was born there, in 1875. Although he lived in Paris, the composer returned to Ciboure to write his famous *Boléro*.

Cap Béar is one of the rocky headlands of the Côte Vermeille (*preceding pages*).

Nestling between the pine forests of Les Landes and the Gironde River, Pauillac (*above*) is regularly visited by those exploring Haut-Médoc. As devotees of fine Bordeaux wines will be aware, the route is studded with châteaux bearing such evocative names as Lafite, Margaux, Latour and Mouton-Rothschild. Standing above the town is the château of Pauillac. The town also has a museum, installed in what were formerly cellars, and a reception hall with paintings and sculptures dedicated to Bacchus. Also worth seeing is a collection of labels, engraved by Braque, Masson and Dalí.

'CONCHYLICULTURE': an ugly word to describe an exotic activity, the farming of shellfish, oysters and mussels. The Marennes-Oléron basin has won itself an international reputation, producing some thirty to forty thousand oysters a year. Before discovering the precious resource, the region enjoyed a rather dubious name. In the Middle Ages, its inhabitants relied largely on shipwrecking and looting to provide them with an income. Aliénor d'Aquitaine put an end to such deviant behaviour by enacting, circa 1199, the *Rôles d'Oléron*, the first body of maritime law. Today, there are no wrecks to be found in the ports of Oléron and Marennes, only the boats of the oyster-farmers drifting past low, dazzlingly white houses.

The city of Carcassonne (*preceding pages*) – with appropriate alterations made by Viollet-le-Duc, at the request of the intrepid Prosper Mérimée, the ancient Cathar town is the very picture of pseudo-medieval splendour.

THE SACRED MOUNTAIN of Le Canigou is the symbol of Catalonia. Its dark green and blue-shaded peaks jut out from the Pyrenees mountain range, between the valleys of the Têt and the Tech. In the mid-nineteenth century, Father Jacinto Verdaguer, the author of the poem 'Le Canigou', enjoyed a reputation in the region that was equal to that of Mistral in Provence. His 1866 epic traces the legend of the Comte de Guilfred, founder of the Abbaye de Saint-Martin du Canigou. The latter, although it stands at an altitude of 1,065 metres, is eminently visitable. The Catalans love exercise and get up into the mountains by every possible means: on foot, by bike, on skis and in their jeeps ... Pierre III of Aragon is said to have been the first person to scale the heights of Le Canigou, in 1285. In 1908, a policeman reached the top on horseback, without once setting foot on the ground, which is no mean feat, as the summit is at an altitude of 2,784 metres. For those who are tempted, the ascent begins at Prades and you then follow a winding route which offers splendid views of the Romanesque abbey of Saint-Michel-de-Cuxa, today the home of Cistercian monks. Its twelfth-century cloister boasts particularly fine capitals. After a steep climb, you make for the chalet refuge of Cortalets, at 2,150 metres, situated at the opening of the natural amphitheatre formed by the two spurs to the north of Le Canigou, the Pic Joffre and the Pic Barbet. You are then within striking distance of the top. It is at this vantage-point that the French and Spanish Catalans light the first fires for Midsummer Day, marking the June equinox.

'IN OUR REGION'S HISTORY, Catalonia and the Church are inseparable. From the close reaction between these two elements, our land was created,' said the bishop of Vich, Joseph Torras i Bages, at the end of the nineteenth century. The abbeys are, if you like, evidence of this union. The priory of Serrabone (*opposite*) is an acclaimed example of twelfth-century artistry. A solitary building standing on the narrow plain of the Aspre, it is in fact one of the finest Romanesque monuments in the entire region. Little is known about the canons who lived there until the fifteenth century, but they eventually departed from this already depopulated region, taking their archives with them. For a long time the priory seemed moribund, but now its future is secure, following the restoration undertaken by the Service des Monuments Historiques. You enter on the east side through a low doorway flanked by two marble columns, the capitals of which directly support a Roman arch. The one on the left features a squat figure of Christ, and that on the right, two lion bodies joined to a single head. In the interior over two-thirds of the nave extends a gallery carried on six arches, supported by ten columns with capitals and two rectangular pillars. The whole interior is made of pink marble veined with white and is covered with sculptures of mythical figures, griffons, a centaur, a lion-dragon. The priory also contains a covered gallery with columns and pillars of schist. Hard to believe, as you look up at this severe mountain sanctuary, that it contains such gems.

The cathedral of Sainte-Cécile d'Albi (*above*).

LOURDES IS A STRANGE CITY, hemmed in by mountains. As a place of pilgrimage it is unequalled anywhere in the world. Religion exists here in a curious symbiosis with commerce – the Virgin Mary appears to the visitor at every second in one shop window after another, in the form of statuettes of varying degrees of aesthetic accomplishment. Yet, because of the many cures that have been effected here since the Virgin showed herself to Bernadette Soubirous in 1858, it is also a place where, for many invalids, hope springs eternal. The atmosphere of the town fascinated the naturalist writers. Zola made it the setting for a book charting the spiritual turmoil of a young *abbé* experiencing religious doubt. In *Les Foules de Lourdes*, Huysmans criticized the town's 'haemorrhage of bad taste'. He depicted a bizarre procession of the sick, the old and the ugly, torn between distress and hope. The miracle of Lourdes, Huysmans wrote acidly, is that no infection has become established in that 'odious soup' in which the sick are immersed.

Les Orgues d'Ille-sur-Têt (*preceding pages*) has amazing 'fairy chimneys' rising up out of the Roussillon plain. These are columns of soft rock encased in hard conglomerate.

THE DRY, barren slopes of
the eastern Pyrenees enjoy
a Mediterranean climate,
except that is for the Vallée du
Fenouillèdes, which is a low-lying
corridor running between the rocky
Corbières and the granite massif
of L'Agly. Saint-Paul-du-Fenouillet,
at 267 metres above sea level, is
an exceptionally sheltered spot
surrounded by mountains. Wheat,
oats and vines all flourish in the
valley. The vines are used mainly
for high-quality table wines, the
best-known label being Corbières,
which comes from an area bounded
by the Aude, the Mediterranean
and the fertile strip of the
Fenouillèdes. The wine-growing
cooperatives proudly advertise
their full-bodied, dark red
wines, designated since 1985 as
appellation contrôlée. The oldest
appellation wine in Languedoc-
Roussillon is actually Fitou, the
label a small number of Corbières
communes have been permitted
to use since 1948. This fine ruby
wine must be no less than 12% in
strength and stays in the cask for
a minimum of nine months. Its
producers are also authorized to
produce sweet wines and the
Rivesaltes muscats on which
the region prides itself. Another
fine product of the locality is the
Blanquette de Limoux made by
Benedictine monks at the Abbaye
Saint-Hilaire.

The

Mediterranean

THE MOUNTAIN seemed absolutely still. The heat was suffocating, the scents of the wild plants made me a little giddy. One or two birds, no more. All the animals must have been sleeping, overwhelmed by the sun. It was high summer. I had soon left behind the area with trickles of water. Now it was all dry rock, although vegetation had not yet yielded entirely to stone. It caused me many problems for at every step a thorn bush blocked my path.

Still, I made good progress and after walking for an hour reached the head of this waterless torrent marked on the map. I hesitated there a while, but finally discovered to my right a series of stone slabs, which I scaled. I saw an eagle take off. I found a semblance of a path again further on and sensed I was climbing up towards the plateau. A backward glance through a gap revealed the plain near Gerbaut, but the path twisted and I lost sight of that lovely piece of blue land all trembling with light. I climbed on. Halfway up, I had to stop. I had been walking for two hours. I needed to catch my breath.

I looked at the Luberon. It was a long time since the days when I contemplated it as a child, when this ghost mountain, a land of wild beasts, used to dominate my dreams. Now I had caught up with it; there it was, and I found it even stranger than in the days when I peopled it with wild boar and wolves. Perhaps in some fold of the landscape I would discover the village it had swallowed up, man by man, house by house.

At about four, I emerged onto the plateau, where there was some air. Wasting no time, I headed west. As the going was by now more or less flat, I walked fast. According to my calculations I must have been quite near the village, and I was surprised I still could not see it. 'What will I find?' I thought, and my heart beat faster.

I caught sight of Silvergues at about five o'clock, on a small mound a little lower down. I came to a halt near the end of the plateau.

The village was built on a slope and access to it was by way of a narrow circular valley. At first you could hardly make out the houses – the walls were built into the rock, and all the buildings had formed a single mass following the contours of the land. Shoulder to shoulder, using the walls as reinforcements, they forged their way upwards, short and squat, helping one another climb to the top of the mound where, surmounting a bare rock, there was nothing to be seen but a stone wall and three cypresses.

Nothing moved. No smoke hung in the air; just a deep silence.

My emotion was too strong to permit the luxury of a longer inspection. I climbed down from the plateau through the ravine, found traces of the winding track leading to the village and strode out along it.

But the first houses rose up in front of me as I turned a bend. There were two of them, with a street running between them, perhaps the only street in the village. Standing on broad bases, their shutters still closed, they made me stop and look. They seemed solid and of such great authority that I went on my way feeling there was still something deserving of respect in this old village on which men had turned their backs. As the street rose, you could see, to right and left, other houses – ramshackled – and at the far end a square with a fountain. Not a sound. Wooden shutters torn from their hinges and, at every step, collapsed roofs. Heaps of tiles littered the ground, with big rafters dangling off them. Here and there a strip of wallpaper on a patch of stucco, a cupboard with one or two shelves left inside, a staircase suspended above a sink, leading into space; and everywhere that smell of soot and wet plaster that denotes abandonment and death in human habitations. A tin sign still hung, covered in rust, above a doorway, doubtless that of some tobacconist's or bar. A few houses bore a number, which was just about the saddest thing in the world. I advanced cautiously, overcome by this solitude, and wondered what I would do if there suddenly emerged out of one of these tumbledown cottages the thickset man I had seen in the night at Gerbaut.

Henri Bosco, *Le Trestoulas*

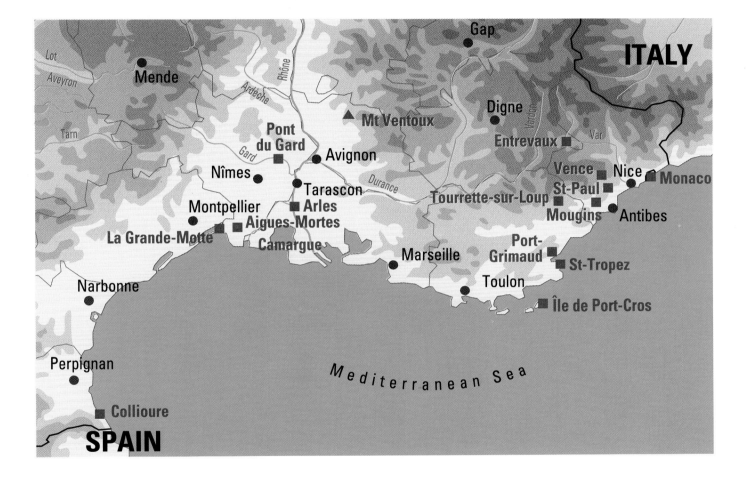

ITALY

Gap

Mende

Lot

Aveyron

Tarn

Ardèche

Rhône

Digne

Mt Ventoux

Verdon

Pont du Gard

Gard

Avignon

Entrevaux

Var

Nîmes

Tarascon

Durance

Vence

Nice

Monaco

St-Paul

Montpellier

Arles

Tourrette-sur-Loup

Mougins

Antibes

Aigues-Mortes

La Grande-Motte

Camargue

Port-Grimaud

St-Tropez

Marseille

Narbonne

Toulon

Île de Port-Cros

Perpignan

Mediterranean Sea

Collioure

SPAIN

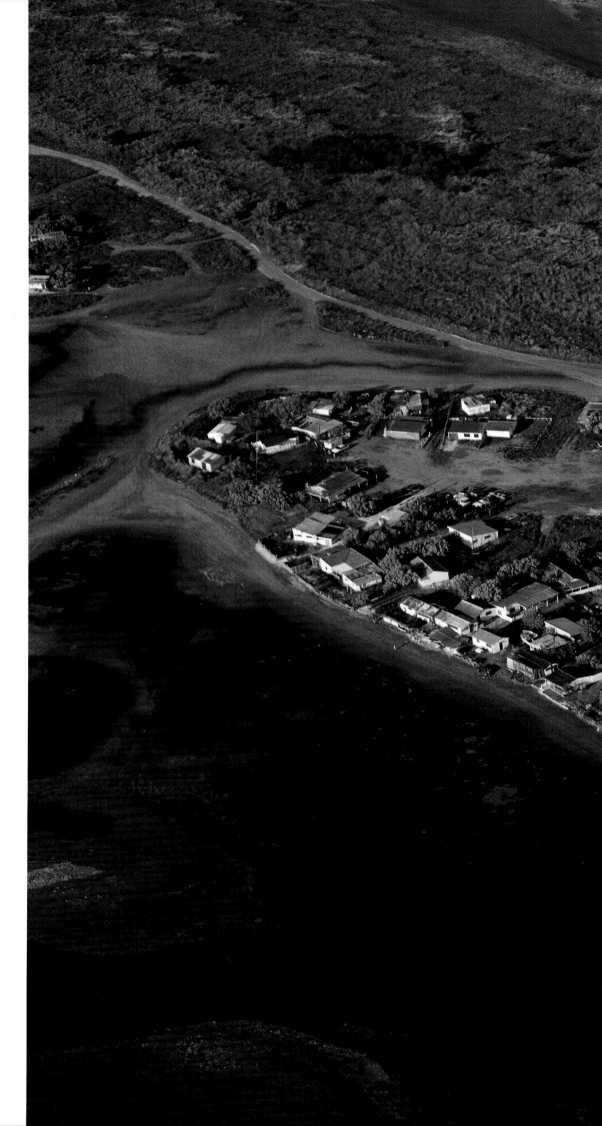

'Marshland fading away into the distance, among the pastures, *roubines* glowing in the saltwort. ... As from the sea, unrelieved despite its waves, so there emanates from this plain a feeling of solitude and immensity, intensified by the mistral which blows unrelenting and unopposed, seeming to flatten and extend the landscape with its powerful blast.' This is how Alphonse Daudet described the wild country of the Camargue. This vast terrain of swamps, pools and salt pastures used to be called the Wild West of Europe. Today, black-and-white horses graze there in cultivated fields ringed with barbed-wire fences, but in the nature reserve at Vaccarès, the Camargue preserves its elemental purity.

From the top of the Pont du Gard, you can contemplate two thousand years of history. The sheer power of the Romans who built this aqueduct is evident. Although their resources were rudimentary, they had an army of slaves at their disposal, who hoisted stones weighing six tons up to a height of over forty metres. Only part of the bridge survives, but originally it extended for 30 miles and was the pride of the Roman Empire. It was built to carry water from the sources of the Uzès to Nîmes. Today, people swim beneath its arches, satisfying an appetite for culture as they picnic on the rocks.

THE AMPHITHEATRE AT Arles is another magnificent Roman monument. The Greeks established this former trading post, which Caesar made one of the capitals of Roman Gaul. Other famous sites include the Romanesque church of Saint-Trophime, dating from the eleventh to twelfth centuries, which has a fine sculpted portal, and the Alyscamps, an avenue lined with sarcophagi. This ancient Roman necropolis is one of the largest in the West. It was a source of inspiration for van Gogh when he stayed in Arles from 1888 to 1899. He loved the town, and amassed more than 300 canvases and drawings.

THERE WAS A TIME, not so very long ago, when Saint-Tropez (*left*, a view of the harbour) was deserted during the summer months. At the end of the last century, Paul Signac painted by the harbour in peace and tranquillity. Dunoyer de Segonzac even published *Saint-Tropézien, le mal connu*. Then the beauty of its situation attracted artists like Matisse and Bonnard. Colette, who loved the colours of the region, bought a little pink house in 1926, on the Route des Salins. She called it 'La Treille muscate' – the title of one of her later books – because of a vine growing by a well. From her small patio, as she wrote in a letter to Marguerite Moreno, she was able to look out on 'the ultramarine sea, pink lilies, vines, blue convolvulus, white clouds'. Colette wrote one of her finest novels while living there, *La Naissance du jour*. The friends she entertained included Cocteau, Paul Géraldy, Francis Carco and Saint-Exupéry. But her presence attracted an influx of sightseers, which forced her to sell her house. In 1956, Roger Vadim chose the town as the setting for *And God Created Woman*, and Brigitte Bardot launched the Saint-Tropez we know today.

THE MONT VENTOUX in Provence (*left*) is much favoured by cyclists and stressed-out intellectuals. The last outpost of the Alps, the mountain reaches an altitude of 1,909 metres, providing a sensational vantage-point from which to view Provence, provided one does not mind the Ventoux wind.

Port-Cros (*opposite*) is a small island classified as a nature park. In this Eden, or 'miniature Corsica' as it was once described, encircled by pine trees and rocky ridges, the warm, balmy air contrasts delightfully with the luxuriant and headily scented vegetation. Along with Porquerolles, which is larger and has many tropical species, and the Île du Levant, a favourite spot for naturists since 1931, Port-Cros forms part of a sheltered archipelago known as the Îles d'Hyères. In its heyday, this stretch of coast backing onto the Maures massif enjoyed a considerable vogue, but the wave of tourism moved on from Hyères to Saint-Tropez and its environs. This has done nothing but enhance the attractions of the area.

The vineyards of the Côtes du Rhône (*preceding pages*).

THE TOWNS Vence, Mougins and Collioure represent the Midi. Many artists have based themselves in Vence (*left*) – a small Roman settlement of Haute-Provence, where lemon trees bloom and gnarled olive branches intertwine. The Chapelle du Rosaire was designed and decorated by Matisse between 1947 and 1951. Matisse regarded this interpretation of medieval art as his masterpiece. In the former cathedral, the oldest parts of the fabric of which date back to the Middle Ages, the tombs of Saint Véran (fifth century) and Saint Lambert (twelfth century), both bishops, are reminders of Vence's episcopal past. Built on the site of a temple dedicated to Mars, the church is an astonishing hotchpotch of styles: Roman sarcophagus, fifteenth-century misericords, sixteenth-century retable, Chagall mosaic, stained-glass windows by Rouault.

In 1961, Picasso went to live in Mougins (*left*), captivated by the beauty of its situation. He remained there with his wife Jacqueline until his death in 1973. His house bears the name 'Notre-Dame de Vie' and stands next to a hermitage at the top of a hill flanked by heavy cypresses. A fabulous spot to live out one's days.

At Collioure (*preceding pages*), Roussillon's main seaside resort, one is almost in Spain. With its ancient royal castle, two colourful fishing ports, the narrow streets of the Mouré quarter and the light of the Côte Vermeille, it has acted as a magnet to painters ever since Braque, Derain and Matisse were regular visitors. The hôtel-restaurant of Les Templiers recalls that golden age with the numerous paintings that decorate its walls.

The rock of Monaco (*opposite*).

'THE PEOPLE have a right to their columns,' Stalin is supposed to have said. At La Grande-Motte, one must suppose, people have a right to their pyramids. The area was nothing but an empty harbour in 1967 when the scheme was inaugurated by General de Gaulle. Ten years later, polyhedrons and towers had sprung from the ground. Some people thought they were having a bad dream when they saw this concrete mass that had appeared in the heart of Languedoc-Roussillon; others were thrilled at the accessibility of beaches, shopping centres and green open spaces. The designers of this 'best of all possible worlds' thought of everything: flowers and trees grow happily between car parks and tower blocks. Resolutely modern, La Grande-Motte satisfies the current requirement for vertical living – its pyramids represent the successful interpretation of that concept. We need only observe the overpopulated beaches near the car parks, while only a few metres away it is possible to be alone, in order to realize the plain fact that tourists abhor a vacuum.

Port-Grimaud (*left*) is a lakeside village that was built in 1966, at the height of Saint-Tropez's popularity.

TOURRETTE-SUR-LOUP, Saint-Paul and Entrevaux are fortified towns in the South of France. Tourrette-sur-Loup (*opposite*) is perched on a rocky plateau. The town rises up above ramparts formed by the houses themselves. It has become a favourite spot for artists, potters and sculptors. Even so, the craft frenzy does not match that of Saint-Paul (*below, right*), which seethes like an anthill the moment summer arrives. One of its curiosities is the auberge-gallery La Colombe d'Or. It was made fashionable in the twenties by painters such as Signac, Bonnard, Soutine and Modigliani, and was later patronized, at different times, by Prévert, Pagnol, Clouzot and Yves Montand and his wife Simone Signoret. But the principal attraction of Saint-Paul lies one mile above the village, on the Colline des Gardettes. This is the Fondation Maeght, a showcase for modern art which is well stocked with the works of Calder, Giacometti, Braque, Chagall and Miró. The opening address was given by André Malraux in 1964: 'Here something is being attempted that has never been attempted before, and that is to create a world in which modern art can take its place and at the same time discover that hidden world once described as the super-natural.' Entrevaux (*above, right*) is in the upper valley of the Var. The houses huddled at the foot of the steep hill are connected by Vauban's ramparts to the castle at the top. Access is via the fortified ramp comprising some twenty defensive gates. From this superb vantage-point there is a fine view of the valley, provided one has enough energy left to enjoy it.

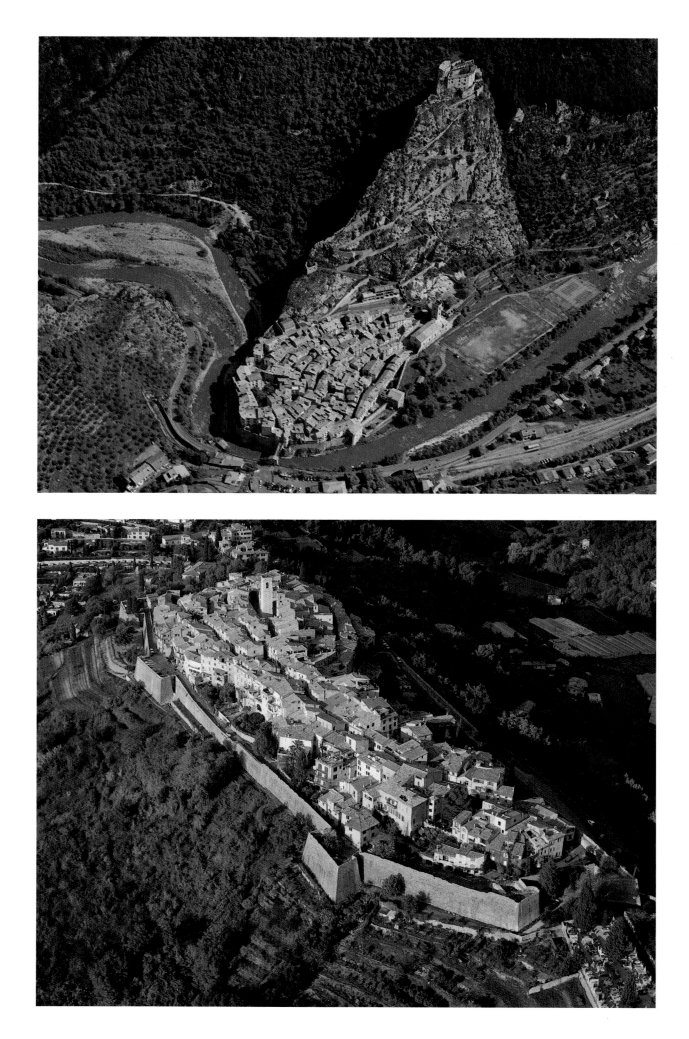

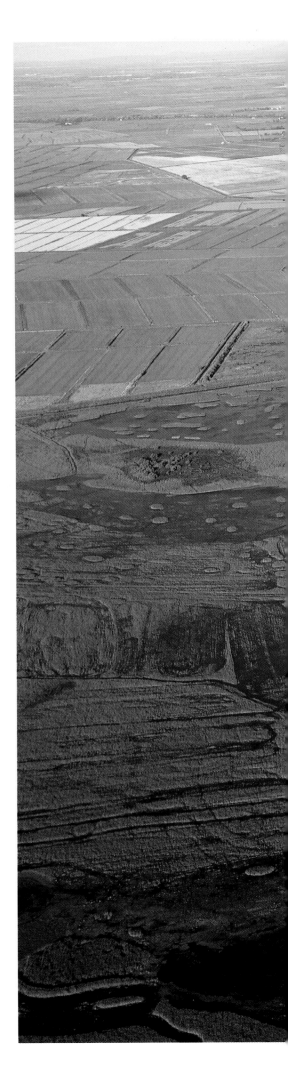

Over the centuries, through the action of the wind and the Mediterranean, the Rhône has formed a vast delta of salt marshes, pools and forests – the Camargue plain. The name evokes a bleak and melancholy landscape populated by horses and pink flamingoes, but, in fact, this popular image corresponds specifically to the area lying to the south of the delta – a sandy waste still protected from the depredations of modern man. The Haute-Camargue, on the other hand, has been worked over since the Middle Ages. Its present-day crops include wheat, maize and rape, and viticulture exists there, as well as market-gardening and fruit-growing. But there is a third area of the Camargue which has been exploited since antiquity, that of the salt marshes and salt pans. These are situated near Aigues-Mortes and Salins-de-Giraud. Even in the twelfth century the monks used to grow fat on their 'salt abbeys'. Industrial techniques were introduced into the region in the nineteenth century and currently the Compagnie des Salins du Midi (based near Aigues-Mortes) is the largest salt-producer in France. It runs tours showing the whole process by which the salt is extracted. The task of reclamation begins once summer is over, and the salt is then washed and stockpiled in *camelles*, or cones, sometimes reaching a height of twenty metres.

Corsica

I WAS UNABLE TO SLEEP last night. The *mistral* was angry, and the sound of its loud voice kept me awake till morning, balancing heavily its mutilated wings, which whistled against the *bise* as through a ship's rigging: the whole mill creaked. The tiles flew away from the roof, routed. The pines, with which the hill is covered, swayed and moaned in the blast. One would have imagined oneself in mid-ocean. It brought me back to my delightful insomnia of three months ago, when I inhabited the lighthouse of the Sanguinaires, down there on the Corsican coast, at the entrance of the gulf of Ajaccio. Still another pretty corner that I had found, where I might dream and be alone. Picture to yourself a reddish island of wild aspect, the lighthouse on one point, on the other an old Genoese tower where in my time an eagle lodged. Below, on the shore, a lazarette in ruins, invaded from all sides by weeds; then ravines and marshes and great rocks, some wild goats and little Corsican horses gamboling, their manes flying in the wind; and above, high up in a whirlwind of sea birds, the dwelling of the lighthouse, with its platform in white masonry, where the guards walk from end to end, the green arched door, the little brass tower, and above it the large lantern cut in facets, which blazes in the sun and seems to give light even during the day – such is the Island of the Sanguinaires, as I saw it again last night, while listening to the moaning of my pines. It was to this enchanted isle that, before I had my mill, I went to shut myself up once in a while when I was in need of solitude and fresh air. What did I do? Just what I do here – even less.

When the *mistral* or the *tramontane* did not blow too hard, I put myself between two rocks, close to the water, among the sea-gulls, the blackbirds and swallows; there I would remain nearly all day in the delicious state of oppression and stupor which the sea gives one. You have felt, have you not, that charming intoxication of the soul? One does not think, neither does one dream; your whole being escapes from you, flies away, is scattered. One is the gull that plunges – the froth of the foam that floats in the sunlight between two waves – the white smoke from the steamer in the distance. ...

The days when a strong wind blew, the shore was not tenable. Then I shut myself up in the court of the lazarette – a melancholy little court, but fragrant with rosemary and wild absinthe: there, crouched against the old wall, I allowed myself to be quietly overcome by the vague feeling of abandonment and sadness which, with the sun, pervaded the little stone cot, open all around like an ancient tomb. From time to time the closing of a door, a light bound in the weeds; it was a goat coming to browse there, sheltered from the wind. On seeing me she stopped, amazed, and stood before me with a wicked air, horns up, looking at me with an eye almost like a child's.

At five o'clock the guard's horn called me to dinner. I then took a little path from the sea, climbing up with a pick, and came back slowly to the lighthouse, looking around at every step upon the vast horizon of light and water, which seemed to grow larger as I made the ascent. It was charming, up on the hill. I can still see the fine dining-room floored with large flag-stones, with a wainscoting of oak, the door wide open on to the white terrace, and the golden sunset coming in. The guards were there waiting for me before sitting at table. There were three of them – one from Marseilles and two Corsicans – all three small and bearded, with bronzed and wrinkled faces, and all wearing the *pelone* (cloak) of goat skin; but their natures were entirely different one from the other. One felt immediately the difference in the two races by their manner of living. The Marseillais, industrious and lively, always busy, always moving; he ran over the island from morning till night, gardening, fishing, picking up gulls' eggs, or lying in ambush ready to milk a goat that might pass by; and always making some *aioli* or some good soup. The Corsicans occupied themselves with nothing outside their service; they considered themselves as functionaries, and passed entire days in the kitchen playing interminable games of *scopa*, only stopping to light their pipes with a sober air, and to cut up the green tobacco in the hollow of their hands with the scissors.

Alphonse Daudet,
Letters from my Mill

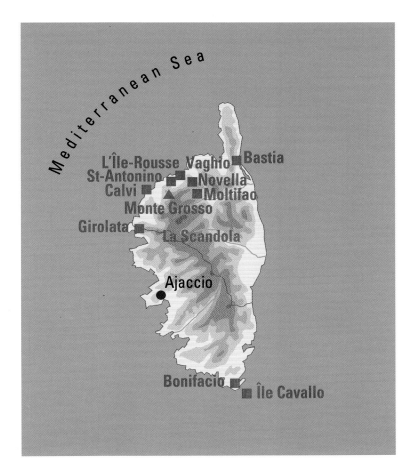

'I HAVE PUT UP THE GALLOWS on which Calvi will hang,' declared Pascal Paoli, as the first houses of the Île-Rousse (*below, left*) were built at his command. In 1758 the 'father of the country' founded *Insularossa*, intending it to be a rival to Calvi, then under Genoese control. Paoli, born in Morosaglia, arrived in Corsica in 1755. He had been a student at the military academy in Naples, where his father and the other rebels were exiled. The 'Genoese peace' that had existed for two centuries was then drawing to a close and the people took up arms and proclaimed their independence. As the appointed general of the Corsican nation, Paoli was the leader of the popular uprising. He gave the island a constitution calculated to impress Enlightenment Europe. Yet the 'revolution' resulted only in France once again taking control of Corsica. Today, some of the islanders are still fighting for their independence; the Place Pascal-Paoli in the Île-Rousse, however, remains the sole preserve of the *pétanque* players. Nowadays, the port, which owes the second part of its name ('rousse') to its red-ochre rocks, is joined permanently to the mainland. Corsica nevertheless remains an island surrounded by other islands. Far away from the modern world, above the Golfe de Girolata and looking out towards the Île de Gargalo, is the nature reserve of La Scandola (*above, left*). Here some of the last fishing-eagles or ospreys can still be seen.

The village of Novella (*opposite*).

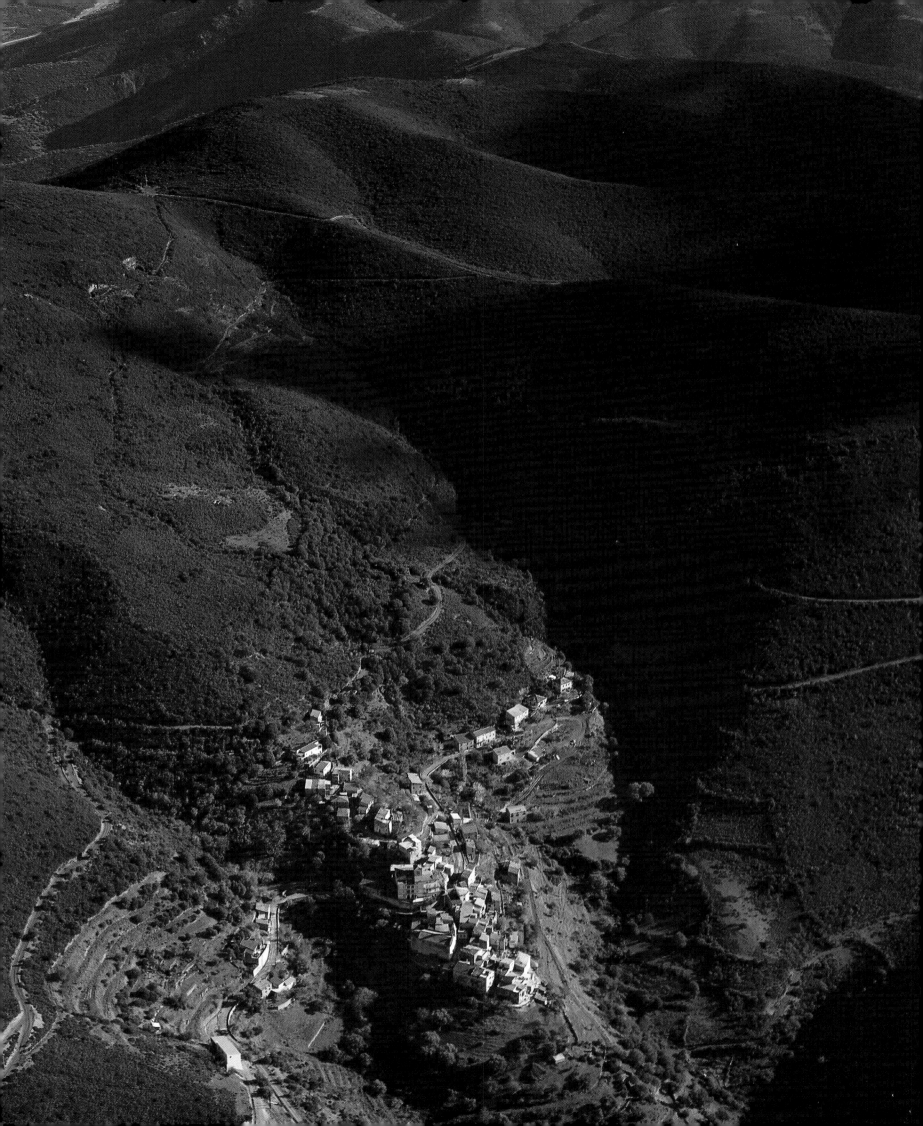

THE ÎLE DE CAVALLO'S resources of grey granite were exploited by the Romans, traces of whose monoliths survive. During the sixties the Corsicans were unhappy when luxury houses were built on the site. On the nearby Îles Lavezzi, a cairn, a chapel and a cemetery commemorate the tragic events of 15 February 1855 when, under the terrified eyes of a shepherd, who was the sole inhabitant, the frigate *La Sémillante* broke up on the rocks. On board were more than 750 men leaving to fight in the Crimea. There were no survivors. This terrible tale inspired an episode entitled 'L'Agonie de *La Sémillante*' in Alphonse Daudet's *Lettres de mon moulin*.

THE ENGLISH christened Corsica the Scented Isle. Napoleon declared he could recognize it just by its smell. In the springtime, an intoxicating medley of scents rises up from the *maquis*, a bouquet of thyme, rosemary, heather, marjoram, lavender, asphodel and honey-suckle. This thorny scrub covers nearly two-thirds of the island, invading cultivated land and areas of burnt forest and depleting the soil. The *maquis* is particularly profuse in the lower reaches of the Asco valley (*preceding pages*, Moltifao).

Bastia (*above*), the island's former capital, is set between sea and mountains on the island's northern tip. This is Cap Corse, or the 'finger of Corsica', which points towards mainland France.

Perfumed by eucalyptus and tamarisk, the beach at Girolata (*below*) is idyllic. The village stands on a promontory, practically inaccessible because of the surrounding *maquis*. It may be reached by boat from Calvi or Porto, or by mule-path. The difficulty of access is of course a major asset because an atmosphere of unbroken peace prevails.

Corse-du-Sud. On the southern tip of the island, apparently barely clinging on, is Bonifacio (*overleaf*), almost a small principality in its own right. Having been colonized by the Genoese in the late twelfth century, the inhabitants retained certain privileges over the years. The town is said to be older than Homer, and Victor Bérard, a Homeric specialist, situates Canto X

The Monte Grosso massif (*left*) is adjacent to the highest of the Corsican peaks, Monte Cinto, which rises to 2,706 metres. The central mountain range dictated the historical division of the island: north of the mountains is Haute-Corse, while the region below is

of the *Odyssey* in the straits of Bonifacio, the land of the Laestrygonian giants. Dominated by the old fort, enclosed on its landward side by the Porte de Gênes and its drawbridge, Bonifacio seems well situated to resist modern development.

THE MOTTO OF THE capital of the region known as the Balagne (*opposite*) is *civilitas Calvi semper fidelis* ('the city of Calvi is always loyal'). This pledge was made to Genoa, under whose protection the city came in 1289, but there were any number of others to whom the words might have been directed, for Calvi was besieged time and again over the centuries. From the early Christian era up to when it came under Roman rule, it successfully resisted all attempts at invasion, but it was occupied by natives of Pisa from 1077 until it was colonized by the Genoese. Aragon then attempted to seize the town, and after that the papal troops, the French, the Turks and, in the sixteenth century, the Corsican partisans of Sampiero d'Ornano. It is easy to see what attracted all these would-be invaders, for to describe Calvi as the jewel in the island's crown is scarcely to do it justice. The upper town, ringed by walls and surmounted by the fort and former governors' palace (today the home of the Foreign Legion), blends harmoniously with the lower town, with its pedestrianized streets, to create a most pleasing harbourside environment.

Vaghio (*above*) is a beach resort in the region of Saint-Florent.

The village of Sant'Antonino (*overleaf*) offers a fine view over the Balagne.

The Alps

THE TRAVELLER arriving from Sallanches looks down the valley of Chamonix and sees the Arve winding into the distance. Gleaming slate bell-towers of Les Ouches, Chamonix and Argentière – the three parishes between which the territory is divided – appear at distant intervals on the narrow plain. On the left, rising above a natural amphitheatre, brightly splashed with gardens, chalets and cultivated fields, are the fir-tree forest and peaks of Le Bréven, around which the wind furls and unfurls the clouds, like thread on a bobbin. To the right is Mont Blanc, the sharp outline of its contours brilliant against the deep blue of the sky. It rises above the high glacier of Taconaz and the Aiguille du Midi, its thousand crags bristling like a many-headed hydra. Lower down, on the edge of the vast bluish cloak which Mont Blanc trails all the way down to the greenery of Chamonix, is etched the jagged profile of the Glacier des Bossons, its fantastic structure appearing at first sight something utterly incredible and impossible. It is more intricate, certainly, and perhaps more singular even than that strange Celtic monument at Carnac, whose three thousand stones, curiously arranged on the plain, are neither merely stones nor constructions. Imagine enormous prisms of ice, white, green or azure, depending on the sun's ray that strikes them, all jammed close together, assuming a host of different attitudes, some inclined, others upright, their dazzling cones outlined against a background of dark larches. You might say it is a town of obelisks, cippuses, columns and pyramids, a city of temples and sepulchres, a palace built by the fairies for souls and spirits; and I am not surprised that the original inhabitants of this region often thought they saw supernatural beings flitting between the spires of the glacier at the hour when day comes and imparts its lustre to the alabaster of their pediments, its colour to the pearl sheen of their pilasters.

Beyond the Glacier des Bossons, opposite the Chamonix priory, swells the wooded brow of Le Montanvert; and, higher, in the same plane, the two peaks of Les Pèlerins and Les Charmoz appear, looking like those magnificent medieval cathedrals laden with towers and turrets, lanterns, spires, steeples, bell-towers and pinnacles; with the undulating Glacier des Pèlerins flowing between them, like waves of white hair on the mountain's grizzled head.

The picture's background fittingly completes this magnificent ensemble. As the eye plays tirelessly over all the different elements that go to make up the vast edifice of these mountains, it finds objects of admiration on every side – first a forest of giant larches carpeting the opposite end of the valley. Above this forest, the tip of the glacier extends beyond Le Montanvert like a crooked arm, causing its marble blocks, vast sheets, crystal towers, steel dolmens and diamond hills to tilt. The glacier opens onto the plain whence the Arveyron springs as a river, only to expire a mile further on as a torrent. ...

Add to the ensemble of this miraculous landscape the eternal presence of Mont Blanc, one of the three highest mountains on earth, which has that character of grandeur that all great things impart to their surroundings; consider that summit, which is quite literally – I avail myself of the fabulous poetic term – one of the ends of the earth; meditate on this striking accumulation, within such a restricted compass, of so many sights that are without rival, and you will believe as you penetrate the valley of Chamonix, if I may be permitted a trivial expression that nevertheless conveys some idea of what I mean, that you are entering nature's collection of curios, a sort of divine laboratory where providence keeps in reserve samples of all of creation's phenomena, or better still, a hidden sanctuary where all the elements of the visible world are housed. ...

The valleys of the Alps are remarkable in that they are, in a certain sense, complete. Each of them, often within the most confined space, is a world in its own right. All have their own distinctive look, form and light, their own particular sounds. You could almost always sum up in a single word the general impression of their physiognomy. The valley of Sallanches is a theatre; the valley of Servoz a tomb; the valley of Chamonix a temple.

Victor Hugo, *Fragment d'un voyage aux Alpes*

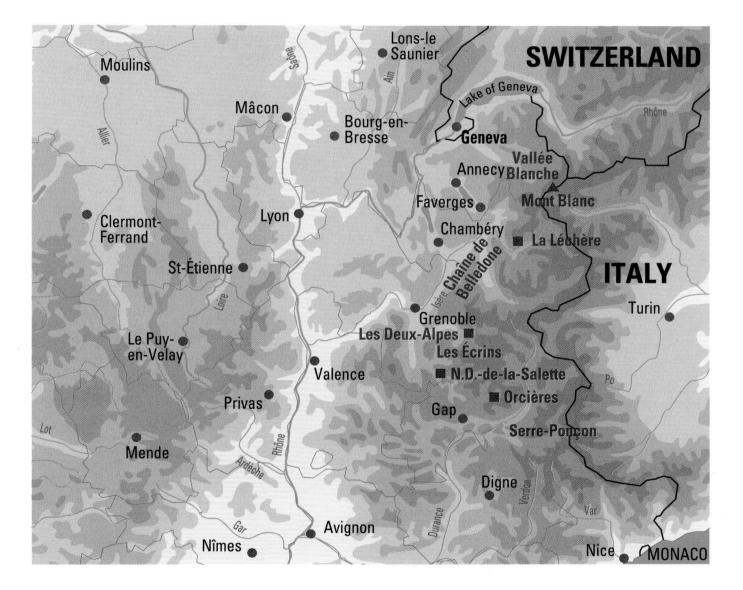

Oᴺᴇ ᴏꜰ ᴛʜᴇ ᴍᴏsᴛ spectacular of man's achievements in the Hautes-Alpes is the dam and reservoir of Serre-Ponçon. Its construction in the sixties involved flooding an area which was more than twelve miles in length and covered over seven thousand acres. The region of Embrun was devastated. Whole villages were sacrificed, submerged for ever beneath the waters. One of these, called Savines, was reborn under the name of Savines-Le-Lac, but the result was a dam which stands 120 metres high. Today, the lake attracts the yachting fraternity. In summer, pilgrims climbing Mont Guillaume can enjoy the sight of tiny crescent-shaped splashes of colour against its blue expanse, contrasting with the austere beauty of the surroundings. A surrealist touch is the little chapel of Saint-Michel on its island at twilight, newly emerged from the waters by which it is regularly engulfed.

'ALP' IS AN ANCIENT WORD meaning mountain pasture. To go up to the alp thus means climbing to a height of some 2,000 to 2,500 metres. The term 'the Alps' is also used to describe a whole region, and refers typically to Tignes, Courchevel, Megève, etc. In other words, places where skiing and winter sports are practised, but the departments of Savoie and Haut-Dauphiné have much more to offer than a series of tourist resorts. They are composed of pretty valleys, old villages and rustic landscapes (*opposite*, the outskirts of Orcières), where a life exists beyond the hurly-burly of the winter visitors. Even the Alps have their seasons – when the snow melts, you can pick the flowers that have bloomed in the light spring showers. At this time of year it is also possible to go canoeing in the rivers, although the sport is not without its hazards if you are unfamiliar with the waters, or there is the more tranquil pastime of fishing for trout. Forget group expeditions and organized trips, the mountain invites meditation, the peaceful solitude of the shepherd. Do the winter sports fanatics actually notice the region over whose *pistes* they swoop in their fluorescent suits? Today, there are signs asking holiday-makers to be careful of the grass, which is needed for the cows. Yet, in a place torn between preserving the habitat and the necessity for economic development, no one will be too critical of the tourist, for he is the goose who lays the golden eggs.

I N THE THIRTIES, the simple act
of putting on skis for the sheer
pleasure of sliding down the side
of a mountain would probably
have been enough to brand you
a half-wit – this is why the first
piste at Alpe-d'Huez was called
the 'idiots' *piste'*. Today no one
would dream of poking fun at this
noble sport, which has brought
prosperity to the region. L'Oisans,
home of the skiing centres of
Alpe-de-Mont-de-Lans and Alpe-
de-Venosc – known collectively as
Les Deux-Alpes (*right*) – has some
of the very best ski slopes. Notably
the huge glacier of Mont-de-Lans,
which commands a fine view over
the whole region. From the domed
top of Le Puy Salié, at an altitude
of 3,421 metres, you can see
inter alia the horse-shoe formation
of the massif of Les Écrins.
Conquered in 1864 by the English
climber Whymper, at its highest
point it reaches an altitude of
4,102 metres, towering above other
peaks of 3,000 metres plus, such as
La Meije, Les Agneaux, Les Bans
and Le Pelvoux. The national park
of Les Écrins was established in
1973, ten years after that of La
Vanoise, and extends over nearly
230,000 acres. Here, among its
fauna, walkers will discover sheep,
chamois and royal eagles, also a
rich flora, for more than 1,800
species have been identified here.
If you pick the blue thistle, Alpine
columbine or genipi, please do not
pull it up by the roots.
   La Léchère (*overleaf*).

In 1941 *Premier de cordée*, the novel by the former alpinist Frison-Roche, was published – who has described better the loneliness and mental anguish of man locked in confrontation with the mountain peaks. With its skiing *pistes* and winter sports resorts, the region may seem to have been tamed, but for climbers it is as tough as ever. These icy heights are entirely without pity, and always will be, as so many of the inscriptions on the tombstones in the cemetery at Chamonix remind us.

La Vallée Blanche (*left*) and the Massif de Belledonne (*above*).

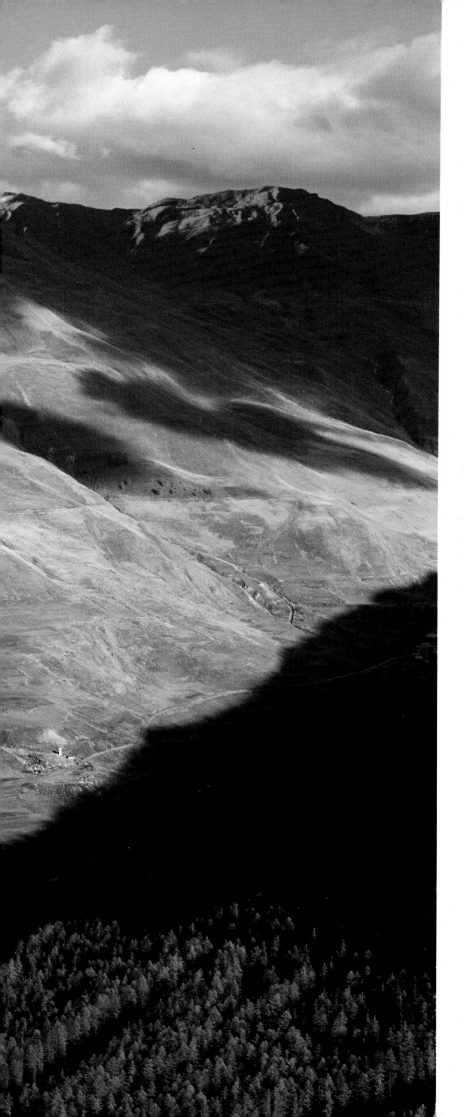

On 19 September 1846, the Virgin Mary appeared to two young children minding sheep, Maximin Giraud and Mélanie Mathieu, aged eleven and fourteen. She wept as she preached a message of conversion, and then disappeared in a halo

of light. The vision of a Madonna in tears is unique in the history of such apparitions. After an investigation lasting five years, the Church accepted the children's account. The basilica of Notre-Dame-de-la-Salette (*above*) was built to mark the spot, a bleak and lonely site in the region of Beaumont, at an altitude of 1,770 metres. (Today, car parks make it more accessible.) Every year since, thousands of pilgrims have climbed up to the sanctuary on the anniversary of the miracle. Just below the sanctuary their path intersects with that taken by other groups of visitors making for Corps, a town on the Route Napoléon. This is the route followed by the emperor on his return from the island of Elba, from the point where he disembarked at Golfe-Juan all the way to Grenoble. It is simply a question of which type of pilgrimage you prefer.

THE MOUNTAINS of the Jura (*left*) are not as high as the Alpine ranges (*overleaf*, Mont Blanc). At an altitude of 450–900 metres, villages huddle among forests of fir trees. The air is stingingly cold, the winters are harsh. The Jurassiens are proud of their region although they tend not to advertise the fact. The writer Bernard Clavel speaks of it with affection, remembering the bread round, going from village to village in a horse-drawn cart with his father, the baker. The Jura had a particular influence on the work of the novelist Roger Vailland. He discovered the Ain valley during the war when he was undercover. It was in his hiding-place at Chavannes-sur-Reyssouze, when cut off from his Resistance network, that Vailland wrote his first novel, *Drôle de jeu*. In 1951 he returned to the area, tired of town life and its temptations, and having by then met his wife Élisabeth. He settled first at Allymes, and then at Meillonnas. The author of *Un Jeune homme seul* wrote his finest work here, in the years before his death in 1965.

The Auvergne

and the Limousin

THE AUVERGNE is famous for its ministers, cheeses and volcanoes. And there's nothing more stark than a volcano. It's like something out of science fiction to see thirty of them clustered around the Puy de Dôme, with that hole in the top of their heads that's like a chicken's nest or a fontanelle that hasn't closed. You would think you were on the moon. It's enough to give you hallucinations.

Goats nibble away on a sort of porous pumice stone (low in nutrient value, however), which gives their somewhat rough-tasting milk just a hint of earth shake – much appreciated by geologists. From this we may deduce that, since the time of the Gauls, the Auvergnats have stopped being afraid the sky is going to fall down on their heads. Perhaps that's because they invented the umbrella and they haven't let go of it since. They have a superstitious feeling about it that is positively British – especially in trains, where they grip it tightly between their legs. They watch it like a pan of milk on the stove. Waste not, want not, is one of their favourite sayings. Industry thrives on it.

They certainly don't waste their volcanoes. The Auvergnats have used them to heat the water underground, making it more commercial, and to invent the barometer, which Pascal discovered at the top of the Puy de Dôme (well, roughly speaking); also to erect the ruins of a fearsome temple dedicated to Mercury, the true god of trade; to show Mont Blanc to tourists and to award the Prix des Volcans.

The Auvergne is physico-chemical. There are carbon gas escapes all over the place; at Royat, in a grotto, a dog was asphyxiated; they showed it to visitors for a small charge, then revived it and started all over again; soldiers got in half-price; that's how scientific know-how gets spread. In the grotto of Saint-Alyre, the water's so chalky it turns dead birds to stone, also donkeys, also Auvergnats (whole Auvergnats, that is, in folk costume), who may be seen dancing the *bourrée* on a lawn, trapped in their stone casings; perhaps the same holds true for bad neighbours? By moonlight, it is an impressive sight. Scientific as well as spectral.

No rivers wind their way through the Auvergne. Here water stagnates in craters eighty metres deep, with the trout and the char, or dashes down slopes in a cloud of spray and evaporates. It scarcely even touches the rock. In Vichy, Châtelguyon, Saint-Nectaire, Saint-Yorre and I suppose La Bourboule and Le Mont-Dore the Auvergnats capture it and put it in bottles which cure complaints of the liver, heart, kidneys, small intestine and other human organs. At Chaudes-Aigues it is used to heat the town. If you break the bottle, you don't get your money back.

What is interesting about the Auvergne is that it is full of Auvergnats. If the latest statistics are anything to go by, there are more here than in Paris. They live on the sides of steep mountains off the products of their fishing, hunting, general savoir-faire and industry; also their water, rubber, cheeses and chocolates and their lace and jam.

They have black hair, eyes like coals, gleaming teeth and layers of jerseys, some maroon, some aubergine, made of thick wool. On 15 August, they remove one layer. On All Saints' Day, they add two more. By the end of their lives they have turned into pure wool; they use grandad as a pin-cushion, and when the doctor listens to his chest he has to peel him like an onion. ...

Go and visit this 'Green Kingdom'. You'll find everything here is on a bigger scale than elsewhere; the wood is darker than anywhere else, the miser more miserly, the grass thicker and the wolf hungrier. You'll hear the wind whistle as you pass 'the good God of Saint-Flour' and look out on vast open spaces smelling of the blue horizon, mushrooms and fir-cones. You will be captivated by an awkward charm it is hard to pin down. For the Auvergne is a battered old piece of furniture long ago despatched by France to the attic. There it has become impregnated with an odour of mustiness, of the olden days, of dreams, of the wood of fir trees. It smells of homespun and smoke. It's more a secret than a province. It's a thought that nags at you. And it is when you have found it that you most want it.

Alexandre Vialatte,
Dernières Nouvelles de l'homme

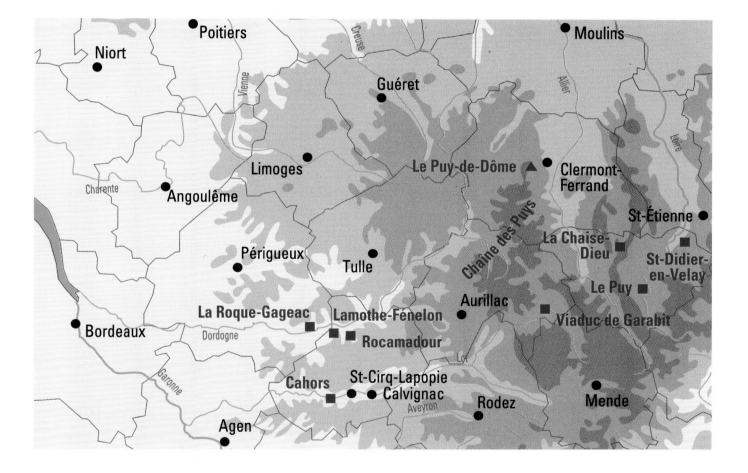

GUSTAVE EIFFEL did more than build a famous tower – among his other constructions is the Viaduc de Garabit (*left*) in the Cantal, 564 metres long and 123 metres high. It was the last project he undertook before embarking on the great Parisian monument. The Dordogne (*above*) starts its journey at the foot of Le Sancy, the tallest peak of the Massif Central. A gushing current, slowed by dams, it proceeds at a brisk rate through the Auvergne and the Limousin. After 300 miles, it joins forces with the Garonne to form the Gironde. It is rightly said that the Dordogne is one of the loveliest of all France's rivers – to go downriver by canoe is the perfect way to appreciate the charms of this ancient land.

IF YOU ARE in the Auvergne, you literally cannot miss the Puy de Dôme: 1,465 metres high, it is the crowning glory of a spectacular chain of volcanoes, the Monts Dômes. On these sacred peaks, which once left the Gauls awe struck, the Romans built a temple to Mercury. Today, a television transmission tower stands there, perhaps as a modern tribute to the gods of communication. There is also an observatory and an institute of geophysics on the spot where Blaise Pascal and his brother-in-law Florin Périer undertook, in 1648, an experiment to prove the law of gravity. Pascal, the most famous of Auvergne's sons, was born at the foot of these extinct volcanoes, at Clermont. That was in 1623, shortly before Louis XIII united the town with Montferrand. Today, the Musée du Ranquet in Clermont-Ferrand has one room devoted entirely to the author of *Les Pensées*, and an exhibition including an example of his famous calculating machine, the 'Pascaline'.

THE MOUNTAINS of the Auvergne may once have been regarded with superstitious awe, but now they are an important part of the region's prosperity, providing many opportunities for excursions and for sport. French paragliding was born in the Chaîne des Puys in 1922, and the many pools in the region are popular with windsurfers. The Parc National des Volcans d'Auvergne also helps promote tourism in the province, and thus maintain the original population of some eighty thousand. The 800,000-acre site, opened in 1977, is the largest of the French national parks.

Budding geologists will discover here a wide variety of volcanic forms, in particular the Peléan and Strombolian types (the Puy Pariou [*above*] is one of the finest cratered volcanoes in the Chaîne des Puys). Hikers and ramblers are amply catered for in terms of overnight accommodation and well-signposted routes.

IN THE ELEVENTH CENTURY, Robert de Turlande determined to retreat from the world and built the original monastery on the plateau of La Chaise-Dieu (*right*). The present abbey, rebuilt by Pope Clement VI, dates from the fourteenth century. In Rocamadour (*below*), which clings precariously to the cliff-face of the Alzou canyon, a perfectly preserved body was discovered in the twelfth in the *langue d'oc* of *roc amator*, which later became Rocamadour. The pilgrimage to this spot became one of the most important in medieval Christendom, but the treasures the town amassed were the cause of its downfall. During the French Wars of Religion, the Huguenots plundered the buildings and tried to burn the body of the saint. Seeing it resist the flames, one Capitaine Bessonies lost his

century, buried under the Chapelle de la Vierge. Since then, many miracles have been associated with the saint's remains. He is said to have been a hermit who lived under a rock. Hence his name temper and smashed the body with a hammer. The pilgrimage to Rocamadour was not revived until the nineteenth century.

The château of Lamothe-Fénelon, in the Périgord (*preceding pages*).

LA ROQUE-GAGEAC is one of the Dordogne's most picturesque towns. Among its many attractions is the charming gabled manor house that was the birthplace of a great sixteenth-century humanist, Jean Tarde. A historian, geographer, astronomer and mathematician, he was canon at Sarlat, where another distinguished humanist first saw the light of day: La Boétie, author of *Le Discours de la servitude volontaire*. Another of his claims to fame was his friendship with the famous Montaigne, who said of him: 'If I am pressed to say why I liked him, I feel there is no other way to express it than by saying, "Because it was him and because it was me".'

CAHORS WAS FORMERLY the capital of Quercy and the leading banking city of medieval Europe – thanks to the Lombard merchants and later the Templars who established themselves there. *Cahorsin* actually became the accepted synonym for usurer.

Saint-Michel at Le Puy (*below*), perched like an eagle's nest on the top of a volcanic cone. It is possible to climb the 268 steps to its mosaic-covered gateway. On top of the town's other extinct volcano, the Rocher Corneille, stands a red-painted statue of the Virgin Mary.

The Hundred Years War laid waste the land but spared the Pont Valentré (*left*), a fine fourteenth-century monument whose arches span the River Lot. With its three machicolated turrets, this feat of medieval military architecture so impressed the English that they left it intact. Another building that is unique of its kind is the Chapelle

The former capital of the Velay also boasts a Romanesque basilica, Notre-Dame du Puy, the chancel of which houses the famous Black Virgin. The statue's canopy is made of the first lace ever to be produced in Le Puy. Sadly this ancient industry is now only a craft activity.

Saint-Didier-en-Velay (*preceding pages*).

Burgundy

MY NAME is Claudine, I live in Montigny. I was born here in 1884, but it's probably not where I'll die.

My *Textbook of Departmental Geography* reads as follows: 'Montigny-en-Fresnois, a small and pretty town with 1,950 inhabitants, forms an amphitheatre above the Thaize; notable features include a well-preserved Saracen tower.' Well, this description means absolutely nothing to me! Firstly, there's no such thing as the Thaize. Oh I know it's supposed to run through some fields below the level crossing, but at no time of the year would you even find enough water to wet the feet of a sparrow. Montigny forms an 'amphitheatre'? It doesn't look like that to me; the way I see it, it is houses tumbling all the way down from the top of the hill to the foot of the valley. The levels form a stairway below a huge castle, rebuilt in the time of Louis XV and already more of a ruin than the Saracen tower, which is low, broad-based and totally covered in ivy, with more and more of the top crumbling away every day. It's a village, not a town. The streets, thank God, are not paved; the rain runs down them in little torrents which dry up in a couple of hours. It's a village, and not even a particularly pretty one, but I just adore it.

The great charm and attraction of this area of hills and valleys, sometimes so narrow as to be ravines, is its woodland, the deep woods that encroach everywhere, rolling away as far as the eye can see, undulating into the distance. ... They are interspersed here and there with green fields and little cultivated patches, nothing much, as the woods simply devour everything. The result is that this beautiful region is horribly poor, its scattered farms few in number, with just about enough red roofs to set off the velvety green of the woods.

Darling woods! I know them all, I've tramped through them so often. There are the copses, with shrubs that lash out viciously at your face as you pass by, they are full of sunlight and strawberries and lily-of-the-valley, and snakes. There I have shuddered with suffocating panic at the sight of those awful smooth, cold little bodies slithering in front of my feet. Twenty times I have stopped and gasped as I discovered under my hand, by the hollyhock, a perfectly docile grass-snake, neatly coiled in a spiral, head on top, its little golden eyes looking at me; not dangerous, but what a fright it gave me! Too bad, I always ended up going back,

either on my own or with friends; usually on my own, because those big babies get on my nerves, either it's afraid of scratching itself on the brambles, or it's afraid of creepy crawlies – the velvet caterpillars, the spiders in the heather, so pretty, round and pink like pearls – or it's crying because it's tired, quite intolerable. Then there are my favourites, the tall timber trees, sixteen or twenty years old, my heart bleeds when I see one cut down; no brushwood here, tree-trunks like columns, straight pathways where it's almost dark by midday, where your voice and your footsteps echo in a scary way. God, how I love them! I feel so alone there, gazing blankly into the distance through the trees, in the mysterious green light, wonderfully peaceful and at the same time slightly anxious, because of the solitude and the murky darkness. ... No creepy crawlies in these tall woodlands, no high grass, but beaten earth, either dry and echoing, or made soft by springs; rabbits with white tails run about in them, and timid deer that move so fast you can only sense they were there; big heavy pheasants, red and gold; wild boar (I never saw any); wolves – I heard one at the start of winter when I was collecting beech-nuts, those lovely little oily beech-nuts that scratch your throat and make you cough. Sometimes there are rainstorms that take you by surprise among the tall trees; you crouch down under an oak that is thicker than the rest and listen in silence to the patter of the rain above, as if on a roof, safely under cover, and emerge later out of the depths all dazzled and disorientated, uncomfortable in the daylight.

And the fir plantations! Neither very deep nor very mysterious, I like them for their smell, for the pink and violet-coloured heather that grows underfoot, and for the song they sing in the wind. The way there is through dense forest, then suddenly you have a wonderful surprise as you come out on the edge of a lake, a deep smooth lake, surrounded on all sides by woodland, miles from anywhere! The fir trees grow on a sort of island in the middle. You have to be bold and shin across using an uprooted tree trunk that links the two banks.

Colette,
Claudine à l'école

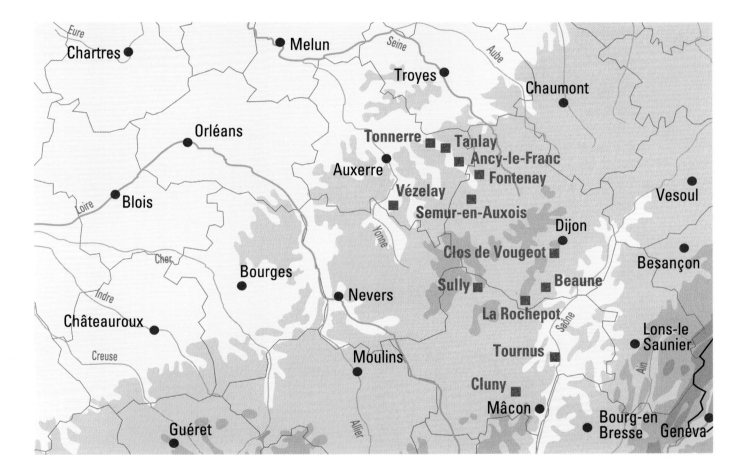

THE CHÂTEAU of Ancy-le-Franc is an elegant tribute to the Italian Renaissance. In 1546, Antoine III de Clermont-Tonnerre, Diane de Poitiers's brother-in-law, commissioned the Bolognese architect Sebastiano Serlio to design the château and Primaticcio and his pupils to carry out the decoration. The result is a measure of Clermont-Tonnerre's good taste, for the severity and plainness of the building are purely external. As you enter the internal courtyard, with its niches and black marble plaques, you are instantly struck by its air of elegance and sophistication. Between the ground-floor pilasters appears the motto of the Clermont-Tonnerres: *Si omnes ego non* ('If all have denied you, I have not'). This is a reference to the fact that in the twelfth century the Comte Sibaud de Clermont helped the Burgundian Pope Calixtus II to resume his position at the time of the Investiture Contest. As a mark of his gratitude, the latter authorized him to display on his coat of arms the papal tiara and keys. Also of interest is the immense hearth in the Salle des Gardes, decorated with *fleur de lys*, and the murals in the Galerie de Pharsale et des Sacrifices. In 1684, the château was bought by Louvois, one of Louis XIV's ministers, but was subsequently reacquired by the family. On the death of the last duke, it passed to his nephews, the Princes de Mérode.

Sénonais, Gâtinais, Puisaye, Nivernais, Morvan, Auxois, Charolais, Dijonnais, Mâconnais, Bresse – Burgundy is made up of a number of smaller regions, each with its own distinct character. There are forests, chalky plateaux, green fields and, of course, vineyards everywhere – the historical basis, we are frequently told, of Burgundian unity. The monks, and notably the Cistercians, have widely been held to bear a major share of responsibility for the deforestation of the area. In his *Histoire de la campagne française*, Gaston Roupnel somewhat qualifies this theory – Cistercian farming, he maintains, was not so much agricultural as concentrated on animal husbandry. Any work of reclamation centred more on the marshes than the forests, and consisted principally of building dykes to hold the waters at bay. If the monks did clear a number of valleys, it was in order to establish the fertile fields on which the region's prosperity depends to this day.

The château of Sully (*above*), in the austere Autun countryside, was built in the Renaissance style.

THE PINK LIGHT from the
stained-glass windows of
Tournus (*above*) casts a soft glow
over the tomb of Saint Valérien,
a Christian martyr who arrived
from Asia Minor as an evangelist.
The sanctuary built to hold his
remains first came to prominence
in the ninth century when it
was occupied by the monks of
Noirmoutier, in flight from the
Normans. They brought with
them the relics of Saint Philibert,
who lent both his name and fame to
the abbey. The foundation suffered
many reverses. It was besieged by
Hungarians in the twelfth century

and abandoned by the priors.
They returned, when charged to
do so by the council, and rebuilt –
but, unhappily, the same pattern
was to be repeated again and
again. Today's visitors can still,
however, explore the church of
Saint-Philibert. Another regular
pilgrimage is to the abbey of
Vézelay (*overleaf*). It is here
that pilgrims used to gather before
setting out for Compostelle. Sacked
by the Huguenots in the sixteenth
century, then partially destroyed in
the Revolution, the buildings were
restored in the nineteenth century
by Viollet-le-Duc.

THE AREA described by Michelet as 'lovely, winy Burgundy' still cherishes the memory of its days of glory under the dukes of Burgundy. In 1363, Philippe II, the Bold, fourth son of Jean II, the Good, received the duchy as his birthright.

Armagnacs, then Philippe the Good and Charles the Bold. The fortune and magnificent lifestyle of the holders of this title won them the name of Grand Dukes of the West. In the fourteenth century Semur-en-Auxois (*left*) was the duchy's

He married the immensely rich heiress Marguerite of Flanders, becoming the most powerful prince in the Christian world. His rise marked the beginning of the prosperity of the Burgundian states. He was succeeded by his son Jean the Fearless, who fought the

stronghold. Because of its forbidding appearance, local legend attributes its building to Hercules. Although plundered by Louis XI, the town retains much of its former grandeur.

The château of Tanlay (*above*) is a Renaissance jewel on the banks of the Armançon River.

'BETTER A LITTLE WINE taken out of necessity, than a lot of water out of greed,' we read in Chapter XI of the *Rule* of St Benedict. We owe so much to the pioneering monks of Burgundy, makers of the best wines in the whole of France. So strong are the links between wine and the monastic life that each order has at least one label to its name. Wine also enjoys a fruitful partnership with art in this region; there is, for example, in the splendid town of Beaune (*right*), a Musée du Vin de Bourgogne which houses a sixteenth-century painting of a Virgin with grapes. The vineyards of Nuits and Beaune were cultivated first by the Romans and then by the Cistercian monks of Cîteaux, the monastery that Saint Bernard entered in 1112, and from where he conducted his campaign against the creeping laxities of Cluny. The future abbot of Clairvaux was a shining light of his age. 'All regarded him as an exceptional man,' we learn from the *Lives of the Saints*, 'while he regarded himself as the lowest of the low.'

THROUGHOUT THE MIDDLE AGES, the name of Cluny (*above*) acted as a beacon to the Western Christian world. 'You are the light of the world,' said Urban II to Saint Hugues in 1096. It was the latter who laid the first stones of the abbey church which was to be completed by his successor Pierre the Venerable. The might deployed by Cluny was moral, material and political, with no less than 1,400 dependent monasteries under the Benedictine abbey's control. Its influence is to be seen in the architecture of numerous churches in Burgundy, such as Paray-le-Monial, built by order of Saint Hugues, La Charité-sur-Loire

and Autun. But Cluny's riches were also its downfall. The abbey and its huge library were sacked during the French Wars of Religion, and the Revolution completed the work of profanation. All that is left today is the transept, the tower of the abbey church and an eighteenth-century cloister. At Fontenay (*opposite*), on the other hand, plainness and sobriety are the order of the day. The plans for the abbey were drawn up by Saint Bernard and the twelve monks who founded the hermitage, situated in a valley near the source of the Seine. Note the marked difference between the Cistercian style of architecture and Cluniac love of ostentation.

THE TOWN OF TONNERRE
(*left*) is linked forever with
the name of a curious individual
known as the Chevalier – or
possibly Chevalière – d'Éon,
born there in 1728. Charles de
Beaumont, to give him his true
name, owes his fame to the aura
of sexual ambiguity that clung to
him all his life. Louis XV sent him
on a diplomatic mission to Russia
where, legend has it, Éon held the
post of reader and lady-in-waiting
to the Empress Elisabeth. Be that
as it may, the Chevalier certainly
took part in the negotiations
that culminated in 1756 with
the ratification of the first Treaty
of Versailles by the empress.
He fought in the Seven Years
War and then went to London,
whence he conducted a clandestine
correspondence with Louis. Back
in France in 1777, the Chevalier,
we are told, decided never again
to take off his woman's clothes.
Hence the controversy that
continued to surround him, but
the autopsy of his body in 1810
revealed that the Chevalier was
indeed a man.

IF THERE IS ONE POET whose name is linked with Burgundy, it is Lamartine. The Romantic writer, born in Mâcon in 1790, was passionately devoted to his homeland, and for that reason continued to be widely read in

took him to their hearts. 'There was no village cabinet-maker, no joiner, no shopkeeper who had not taken out a subscription to receive part issues of these works, which nowadays only educated people would be familiar with.'

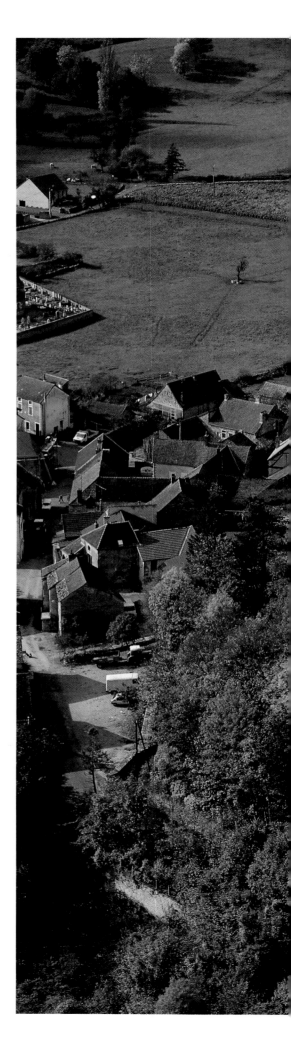

the area – so at least we are informed by Henri Vincenot in *La Billebaude*, his reminiscences of an Auxois childhood. Lamartine's works were published in popular editions between the years 1850 and 1870, and the Burgundians

The château of La Rochepot (*right*) was built in the twelfth century, remodelled in the fifteenth – it is one of the most beautiful reminders of the golden age of the dukes of Burgundy.

IT WAS NOT simple vanity that made the dukes of Burgundy describe themselves as 'lords of the best wines in Christendom'. The Côte de Beaune produces great red wines, such as Pommard at Volnay, and whites like Meursault and Puligny-Montrachet. Mâcon has its legendary white, Pouilly-Fuissé, and L'Yonne can pride itself on the products of the Chablis region. As for the Côte de Nuits, its estates read like a litany of fine vintages: Gevrey-Chambertin, Morey-Saint-Denis, Chambolle-Musigny, Nuits-Saint-Georges and Clos-de-Vougeot, the most prestigious of the Burgundies. The priory of Clos-de-Vougeot (*right*) was built in 1110 by Cistercians. They also planted the surrounding vineyards, soon to acquire a universal reputation. Courtépée relates that in 1359 the abbot of Cîteaux, Jean de Bussières, presented thirty bottles of this wine to Pope Gregory XI. As a mark of his gratitude, His Holiness made him a cardinal four years later. Clos-de-Vougeot remained the property of the Cistercians until the Revolution. Since 1944, the château and its 120 acres of vines have belonged to the confraternity of Le Tastevin, which has become known the world over since its foundation in 1934. Each year, the estate's vast cellars accommodate five hundred guests who perform ceremonies involving the most solemn rituals. Their motto 'Qui boit bon vin, Dieu voit' may be roughly translated as 'God looks kindly on the man who drinks good wine'.

Alsace

Yesterday I visited the church. The Münster is truly a marvel. The church portals are handsome, particularly the Roman portal, on the façade are most superb figures on horseback, the rose window is noble and well carved, the entire front of the church is a subtly orchestrated poem. But the real glory of this cathedral is its spire, with its crown and cross, this is a veritable papal tiara in stone, a prodigy of giganticism and delicacy. I have seen Chartres, I have seen Antwerp, I needed to see Strasbourg.

The church was never completed. The apse, miserably truncated, was contrived according to the taste of the Cardinal du Rohan, that imbecile of a man involved in the scandal of the necklace. It is hideous. The stained-glass window installed there bears a design frequently seen on carpets. It is vile. The rest of the windows are handsome, except where the stained glass has been replaced, notably in the great rose window. The whole of the church is appallingly painted: some of the sculpture has been restored with a modicum of taste. In this cathedral, everyone has had a finger in the pie. The pulpit is a small fifteenth-century edifice in flamboyant Gothic, ravishing in design and style. Unfortunately it has been gilded in a quite stupid fashion. The font is of the same period, and its restoration superior. The vessel positively bristles with the finest sculptures in all the world. To one side, in a dark chapel, are two tombs. One, that of a bishop in the age of Louis V, is the embodiment of that awesome notion Gothic art sought to express in all its manifestations: a bed, and beneath it a tomb, sleep superimposed on death, man on a corpse, death on eternity. The sepulchre occupies two levels. ...

The church seen, I climbed the bell-tower. You know my penchant for perpendicular explorations, I would scarcely have been likely to miss the world's tallest tower. The Münster at Strasbourg is nearly five hundred feet high. It is the type of tower where access is by open stairs. What a wonderful thing it is to move freely through this monstrous mass of stone, flooded with air and light, hollowed out just like one of those little carved knick-knacks from Dieppe, lantern and pyramid alike, shaking and rattling with every gust of wind. I climbed to the top of the vertical steps. As I was going up, I met a visitor on his way down, all pale and trembling, half carried by his guide. Yet it is not in the least dangerous. Any danger there might be started at the point where I stopped, at the foot of the spire proper. ... No guard-rails, or nothing to speak of. The entrance to this stairway is closed off by an iron gate. This gate is opened only with the special permission of the mayor of Strasbourg, and you cannot go up unless you are accompanied by two roofers, who fasten a rope around your body and attach the other end of this at intervals, as you climb, to the iron bars across the window apertures. A week ago, three women, German, a mother and her two daughters, made this ascent. ...

From where I was standing, there was a wonderful view. You are so high up that the landscape ceases to be a landscape; it is, like the sight that greeted me from the mountain at Heidelberg, a geographical map, but a living map, with mists and puffs of smoke, light and shade, gleams of water, flickering leaves, clouds, rain and sunshine.

The sun is only too pleased to put on a display for people looking down from a great height. Just at the very moment I was on the Münster, it suddenly parted the clouds that had covered the sky all day and set alight all the puffs of smoke above the town, all the mists on the plain, at the same time shedding a golden rain over Saverne, whose magnificent slopes I glimpsed once more, twelve leagues away on the horizon, through a glittering veil. Behind me, a thick cloud was raining down on the Rhine; the town lay peacefully at my feet, and its words were carried to me on gusts of wind; the bells of a hundred villages rang out; brown and white aphids – a herd of cows – mooed in a field to the right; other blue and red aphids – gunners – carried out firing practice on the range to the left; a black beetle – a coach – ran along the Metz road; and to the north, on the brow of a hill, the castle of the Grand-Duc de Bade sparkled like a precious stone in a pool of light. I just went from one turret to another, in this way contemplating in turn France, Switzerland and Germany, all in a single sunbeam.

Victor Hugo,
Le Rhin, in *Voyages*

WALKING ALONG BY THE Rhine, you can see, dotted all along the ridges of the Vosges, the ruins of fortifications constructed by the military engineer Vauban – the seventeenth-century Marshal of France. Towards the end of the century, he built the fortified town of Neuf-Brisach (*left*), east of Colmar. It is patterned on a square grid, so that, extending outwards again in the Second World War, the ramparts are well preserved, and it is still possible to walk right round them. There is a museum dedicated to Vauban, showing the scope of his achievements in military engineering and fortification. One could scarcely mention Alsace without referring also to one of its most famous emblems, the white stork – which, sadly, is dying out.

from the central Place d'Armes, which has a well in each of its four corners, the roads intersect to form perfect right angles. Even though they suffered damage in 1870 and

Hunawihr (*above*) has a centre for the preservation of the stork, opened in 1976, a place where the birds can stay all the year round and reproduce in safety.

A N OUTCROP OF SANDSTONE rises out of the green Dabo countryside. The Rocher de Dabo is on the frontier of Alsace and Lorraine, in the Petites Vosges, native region of Erckmann and Chatrian, authors of *L'Ami Fritz*. This legendary rock is set in a romantic landscape, full of deep forests, Romanesque abbeys and ruined feudal castles. There used to be a castle on the Rocher de Dabo, but it was demolished in 1679 and replaced by a neo-Romanesque chapel dedicated to Saint Léon. The latter was born in Eguisheim in 1002 under the name of Bruno de Dabo. His priestly vocation became apparent at an early age, and he was appointed Bishop of Toul before his elevation to the papacy in 1049 as Leo IX; he died in Rome in 1054. His statue is set into the wall of the chapel tower. Apart from its religious and historical interest, the Rocher de Dabo is an excellent observation point – its two viewpoint indicators make it easy to identify the sandstone peaks of the Vosges, and in particular the Donon, which at 1,009 metres is the highest summit. On its heights, it is said, many human sacrifices were made to the Druids, although the Emperor Claudius put a stop to these pagan practices in the Gallo-Roman period. Incidentally, this is also the place where Victor Hugo was conceived. On the day of the summer solstice, large crowds gather to watch the sun rise above the still-sacred mountain.

A PLEASANT WAY to explore Alsace is to follow the Route du Vin from Thann to Marlenheim – particularly enjoyable at the time of the wine harvest. The route extends for some 60 miles, offering prospects of magnificent châteaux as well as delightful villages like Dambach-la-Ville (*left*). With its

region. Viticulture and wine-production have deep roots in this part of the world. And yet a lot of the Alsace wines are not well known, sometimes because their names are difficult to retain. (It is like a tongue-twister – Scharrachbergheim; Niedermorschwihr.)

fortified walls, moat and three defensive gates, it retains a convincingly medieval air. In the third century, the Roman Emperor Probus had the excellent idea of introducing vines to the

Another Alsatian tradition is growing cabbages (*above*). The manufacture and consumption of *saurkraut* is a hallowed tradition in these parts. Alsace is no place for the faint-hearted.

STRASBOURG CATHEDRAL (*below*) is one of the finest examples of Gothic architecture in the whole of France. In 1772, when Goethe was a student in the town, it inspired him to write his famous essay 'On German Architecture'.

and churches, it is as picturesque as any town in Flanders.'

The city of Sélestat (*left*) dates back to antiquity. Local legend has it that it was founded by the giant Schletto and that one of his ribs is preserved there, although it is

The huge edifice made a deep impression on Victor Hugo. He visited it in 1839 and climbed the 328 steps up to the platform of the belfry. He was amazed: 'You have Strasbourg at your feet, an old town with indented gables and big roofs set with skylights. Intercut with towers

probably, in fact, a saurian fossil. Sélestat is regarded as a fount of humanism. Since 1441 there has been a school teaching Latin to generations of scholars. One can still visit the library, which contains a number of priceless manuscripts.

The village of La Petite-Pierre (*preceding pages*).

THE CHÂTEAU OF Haut-Kœnigsbourg (*left*), sometimes described as the Pierrefonds of Alsace, is an extraordinary neo-medieval reconstruction in pink sandstone, which was built between 1901 and 1908, and is the work of the German architect Bobo Ebhardt. The original fortress was much looted and battered before finally falling to Wilhelm II, in 1899. Like Pierrefonds, largely rebuilt by Viollet-le-Duc, it has attracted brickbats as well as bouquets. Its detractors particularly dislike the square keep. The Kaiser posted an inscription on one of the chimney grates in April 1918, which reads *Ich habe es nicht gewollt* ('I wanted none of it'). Some cynics have read this as a *mea culpa* for his architectural folly; he was of course referring to the war. A fairy-tale castle, Haut-Kœnigsbourg remains a great attraction for visitors.

THE CHÂTEAU of Haut-Barr (*above*), in the forest of Saverne, is a magnificent fortress built on three outcrops of rock. Because of the panoramic view it offers, it has been dubbed 'the eye of Alsace'. It was built in the twelfth century, and substantially remodelled over the succeeding centuries by the prelates of Strasbourg. A system of wooden steps and gang-planks enables one to explore it at one's leisure. Two hundred metres from the castle is a reconstruction of the tower once used as a relay station for the aerial telegraph invented by Claude Chappe. This was, quite literally, a revolutionary method of communication, as the first line established between Paris and Lille in 1794 carried the news of the National Convention.

The mountain refuge of Le Honeck, in the Vosges (*opposite*).

THE FORTRESSES OF Lutzel-bourg and Rathsamhausen tower above the village of Ottrot, just north of the Hohwald. Lutzelbourg is a square twelfth-century structure flanked by a round tower, and Rathsamhausen (*right*) was built in the early thirteenth century. A little old-fashioned steam train provides a pleasant means of exploring the local châteaux as far as Rosheim. But Ottrot is also reputed for its vines, and indeed produces one of the best red wines in the region. The village is therefore a welcome stop on the Route des Vins d'Alsace. *Caves de dégustation* are plentiful along the route from Marlenheim to Colmar, passing via Riquewihr, an old city enclosed within medieval walls that produces a famous riesling. Here, since the sixteenth century, most of the inhabitants have been in some way connected with the wine trade. From Colmar the route continues to Thann, where it is said of the local *rangen*, that 'a man cannot stand one jar without being drunk and falling down'.

Katzenthal (*overleaf*).

TITLE PAGES OF CHAPTERS:

INDEX

PHOTOGRAPHIC CREDITS

All the photographs in this book are by Daniel Philippe, with the
following exceptions:
pp. 22–23: Altitude (photo Yann Arthus-Bertrand);
p. 35: Magnum (photo Gaumy);
pp. 95, 96–97, 104–05, 107, 108–09, 112–13, 136, 137:
Explorer (photo F. Jourdan)

Published in collaboration with Renaud Bezombes